Creating Google Chrome Extensions

Prateek Mehta

Apress®

Creating Google Chrome Extensions

Prateek Mehta
New Delhi, India

ISBN-13 (pbk): 978-1-4842-1774-0   ISBN-13 (electronic): 978-1-4842-1775-7
DOI 10.1007/978-1-4842-1775-7

Library of Congress Control Number: 2016943479

Managing Director: Welmoed Spahr
Acquisitions Editor: Ben Renow-Clarke
Development Editor: Matthew Moodie
Technical Reviewer: Massimo Nardone
Editorial Board: Steve Anglin, Pramila Balen, Louise Corrigan, James DeWolf,
    Jonathan Gennick, Robert Hutchinson, Celestin Suresh John, Nikhil Karkal,
    James Markham, Susan McDermott, Matthew Moodie, Douglas Pundick,
    Ben Renow-Clarke, Gwenan Spearing
Coordinating Editor: Nancy Chen
Copy Editor: Kezia Endsley
Compositor: SPi Global
Indexer: SPi Global
Artist: SPi Global

Distributed to the book trade worldwide by Springer Science+Business Media New York, 233 Spring Street, 6th Floor, New York, NY 10013. Phone 1-800-SPRINGER, fax (201) 348-4505, e-mail orders-ny@springer-sbm.com, or visit www.springer.com. Apress Media, LLC is a California LLC and the sole member (owner) is Springer Science + Business Media Finance Inc (SSBM Finance Inc). SSBM Finance Inc is a **Delaware** corporation.

For information on translations, please e-mail rights@apress.com, or visit www.apress.com.

Apress and friends of ED books may be purchased in bulk for academic, corporate, or promotional use. eBook versions and licenses are also available for most titles. For more information, reference our Special Bulk Sales–eBook Licensing web page at www.apress.com/bulk-sales.

Any source code or other supplementary materials referenced by the author in this text is available to readers at www.apress.com. For detailed information about how to locate your book's source code, go to www.apress.com/source-code/.

Printed on acid-free paper

*Dedicated to my parents and my brother for their
everlasting support and encouragement.
And to the Stack Overflow community, for making computer
programming less troublesome.*

Contents at a Glance

Contents at a Glance

Contents

About the Author

Prateek Mehta (pixdip.com/admin/about.html) holds a bachelor's in Information Technology Engineering from the Indraprastha University, New Delhi. He is a web and game developer and is currently working full-time as a Unity3D Game Developer at MetaDesign Solutions, Gurgaon. He finds developing Chrome extensions really fun because he considers extensions the best possible way to enhance browsing experiences. Some of the sample extensions from this book, published on the Chrome web store, are available at pixdip.com/extensions. Prateek resides in the lovely city of Dwarka, in southwest Delhi. When not doing technical things, he works as a freelance music instructor. He spends his spare time playing Counter-Strike. de_dust2 and de_inferno are his favorite maps, where he is busy sniping with his AWP. On Stack Overflow, he has a keen interest in answering questions tagged under "css", "javascript", "php", "unity3d", and "opengl-es-2.0".

He was also the lead author of *Learn OpenGL ES* (Apress, 2013).

About the Technical Reviewer

Massimo Nardone holds a master's in computing science from the University of Salerno, Italy. He has worked as a project manager, software engineer, research engineer, chief security architect, information security manager, PCI/SCADA auditor, and senior lead IT security/cloud/SCADA architect for many years. He currently works as the chief information security officer (CISO) for Cargotec Oyj. He has more than 22 years of work experience in IT, including in the security, SCADA, cloud computing, IT infrastructure, mobile, security, and WWW technology areas for both national and international projects. He worked as a visiting lecturer and supervisor for exercises at the Networking Laboratory of the Helsinki University of Technology (Aalto University). He has been programming and teaching people how to program with Android, Perl, PHP, Java, VB, Python, C/C++, and MySQL for more than 20 years. He holds four international patents (in the PKI, SIP, SAML, and Proxy areas).

He was also the co-author of *Pro Android Games* (Apress, 2015).

Acknowledgments

My sincere thanks go to Steve Anglin and Ben Renow-Clarke for giving me this wonderful opportunity to write for Apress! Thanks to my coordinating editor, Nancy Chen, for handling this project to completion.

Thanks to Matthew Moodie, for his efforts to improve the content, and to Massimo Nardone, the tech reviewer for this book, for providing his helpful insights. Thank you to Tom Welsh and Jill Balzano—the editors on my first book *Learn OpenGL ES*—for mentoring me and preparing me as an author.

Thanks to my friends—Anupam Appar and Pratik Sharma—for reviewing the source code and providing the necessary encouragement to write this book. Also thanks to my pro-gamer comrade, Tejas Tilak, for lending his amazing photography skills.

Introduction

Creating Google Chrome Extensions is an intermediate-level book that teaches development of browser extensions for Google Chrome web browser. Browser extensions are extremely viable in enhancing functionality of web browsers. They have access to almost all the features provided by the browser. And they can encapsulate such features in the form of a bundled application to provide a targeted functionality to users – such as an extension that can summarize the current page you are reading, or another extension that can save all the images in the page you are browsing. Extensions run in a sandboxed environment, making them secure – which is a huge plus!

The APIs provided by Chrome Extensions framework help to empower web applications by coupling them with amazing features provided by the Google Chrome web browser, such as bookmarks, history, tabs, actions, storage, notifications, search, and a lot more other features.

After understanding the examples and lessons in this book, you will be able to transform your existing web applications as (into) Google Chrome browser extensions, as well as create brand new extensions that serve some useful purpose.

In this book we will go from discovering what Google Chrome Extensions are, how to create them, extension components and messaging, to publishing of extensions on the Chrome Web Store (formerly the Google Chrome Extensions Gallery).

"Extensions" is the only way out for sped-up productivity on Google Chrome browsers.

So, showcase your existing web development skills in a completely modernized way, by "Creating Google Chrome Extensions".

CHAPTER 1

▪▪▪

Introduction to Google Chrome Extensions

In this chapter you will learn about Google Chrome Extensions, which are a useful way to add functionality to the Google Chrome web browser. We will first take a quick look at some popular Google Chrome Extensions and the technologies that are used to code Chrome Extensions. Then, you will learn how to create your own "Hello World" style Chrome Extension—but only after we describe the features and abilities of Chrome Extensions. Finally, you will learn about publishing Chrome Extensions on the Chrome Web Store (formerly the Google Chrome Extensions Gallery).

This chapter assumes you have some experience writing simple web pages using technologies such as HTML, CSS, and JavaScript. That said, let's get started!

What Are Google Chrome Extensions?

Google Chrome Extensions are browser extensions for the Google Chrome web browser. Browser extensions are programs that run within the context (security sandbox) of a web browser. They help to provide new functionality(ies) by combining existing features of the web browser and make it possible for users to do many things at once!

▪ **Note**   At the time of this writing, Google Chrome Extensions are only supported on the desktop versions of the Google Chrome web browser.

Support for Browser Extensions

The Google Chrome web browser started supporting browser extensions in its fourth version, which was released in 2010. It is also possible to create extensions for browsers such as Safari, Mozilla Firefox, and Opera. Extensions created for the Google Chrome

---

Electronic supplementary material   The online version of this chapter (doi:10.1007/978-1-4842-1775-7_1) contains supplementary material, which is available to authorized users.

web browser are compatible with the Opera web browser, ever since Opera shifted to the Chromium's extension model (after Opera dropped its own Presto engine, in favor of the WebKit engine used by the Google Chrome web browser, from the Chromium project).

Developing extensions for the Safari web browser has a similar learning curve to that of the Google Chrome web browser, and developing extensions for both is easy because it does not require you to learn any newer technologies (only existing web technologies are used). But developing extensions for the Firefox web browser is comparatively difficult as it involves the use of technologies apart from web technologies, such as XUL, XPCOM, etc. (you can read more about these at https://en.wikipedia.org/wiki/Add-on_ (Mozilla)#Extension_technologies). This book only covers development of extensions on the Google Chrome web browser.

■ **Note**   The Chrome Web Store is an online marketplace where users can browse for Chrome apps, extensions, and themes. The store helps users find, purchase, and install content on the Chrome browser.

Extensions Are Not Plug-ins

An important point to note is that browser extensions are different from browser plug-ins. While browser extensions are sandboxed within the host web browser (software), plug-ins are not. Here, a sandbox can be thought of as a software container – allowing the execution of web technologies, and at the same time providing access to the features of browsers, such as tabs, history, buttons, popups, etc.

In addition to this, extensions add new functionality(ies) to browsers by combining existing features that are already available on browsers (in case of Chrome Extensions, this is done using the API provided by the Extensions framework). Plug-ins, however, provide new functionality(ies) by providing support for particular media types to browsers. In the former case, the example could be an extension that allows users to save all the opened tabs that are not in incognito mode, to the local storage. For the latter case, the example could be a plug-in that allows reading and rendering of PDF files on the browser.

Also note that there is another kind of web application that developers can create for the Chrome browser. These applications are known as *Google Chrome Apps*. From a development's standpoint, Google Chrome Apps are somewhere in between Google Chrome Extensions and browser plug-ins.

This book does not discuss developing Google Chrome Apps, as it only targets the development of Google Chrome Extensions. But keep in mind that developing Chrome Apps is very similar to developing extensions for the Chrome browser. If you want to know more about Google Chrome Apps, you can visit the following URLs:

- https://en.wikipedia.org/wiki/Google_Chrome_Apps

- https://developer.chrome.com/apps/about_apps

- http://stackoverflow.com/questions/tagged/google-chrome-app

Extensions and Plug-ins

To get a complete list of the extensions installed (added) on your Chrome web browser, tab over to the URL chrome://extensions, as shown in Figure 1-1. This page (known as the Extensions Management page) is used to manage extensions in the Chrome browser.

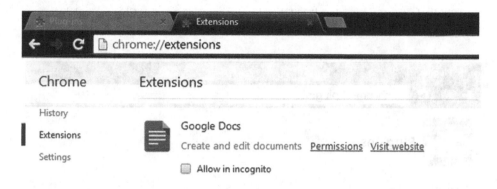

Figure 1-1. *Viewing the Google Chrome Extensions*

■ **Note**   The item in Figure 1-1 (i.e. Google Docs) is not an extension. Instead, it is a Google Chrome App. Both—apps, and extensions—are listed on the same page in the Chrome browser (chrome://extensions), known as the Extensions Management page. Additionally, apps are also listed on the page located at the URL chrome://apps.

Consider pinning this tab (right-click on the tab and then choose the Pin Tab option—see Figure 1-2), as it will be used quite often during the course of this book.

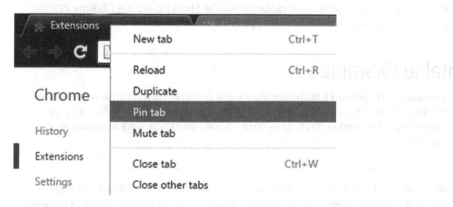

Figure 1-2. *Pinning the chrome://extensions tab*

3

■ **Note** *Sandboxing* is a technique frequently used to test and/or execute unverified programs (which may contain viruses or other malignant code) so that they can't harm the host software.

Similarly, to get a complete list of the plug-ins running on your Chrome web browser, tab over to the URL `chrome://plugins` (shown in Figure 1-3).

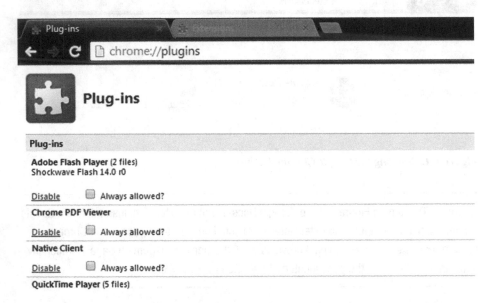

Figure 1-3. *Viewing the Google Chrome plug-ins*

Well-known browser plug-ins include the Adobe Flash Player, the Chrome PDF Viewer, the QuickTime Player, and the Java plug-in.

Notable Examples

As of February 2010, around 2,000 extensions were available on the Chrome Web Store (http://en.wikipedia.org/wiki/Google_Chrome_Extensions#cite_note-4). But surprisingly, as of September 2014, more than 30,000 extensions were available on the Chrome Web Store!

■ **Note** The terms "browser" and "web browser" are used interchangeably throughout this book. Note that they both refer to the same thing, i.e., the desktop versions of the web browser.

Google Chrome users heavily rely on extensions for increasing their productivity at work, enhancing their ability to access the data (already available) on the web, and for getting the most out of their favorite web browser. The following list provides some popular Google Chrome Extensions that are available for free installation from the Chrome Web Store. Note that the usage statistics provided are as of March 2016:

- Adblock Plus—10,000,000+ users
- AddThis: Share & Bookmark—600,000+ users
- Awesome Screenshot: Capture & Annotate—900,000+ users
- Evernote Web Clipper—4,500,000+ users
- Google Dictionary—3,000,000+ users
- Google Translate—6,000,000+ users
- Hangouts—6,500,000+ users
- LastPass: Free Password Manager—4,000,000+ users
- Photo Zoom for Facebook—1,500,000+ users
- Pin It Button—10,000,000+ users

■ **Note**   To view all the (free and paid) Google Chrome Extensions available on the Chrome Web Store, visit the URL https://chrome.google.com/webstore/category/extensions.

Adding Extensions from the Store

It is extremely easy to add extensions available on the Chrome Web Store to your Chrome browser. First of all, you need to visit the extensions' store, located at the URL https://chrome.google.com/webstore/category/extensions. Once you are in the store, you can choose any extension(s) that you want to add to your Chrome browser.

Next, on the selected page you need to click the Add to Chrome button as displayed in Figure 1-4.

Figure 1-4. *Adding an extension from the store*

Finally, click on the Add Extension button (Figure 1-5) to confirm your selection. Congratulations, you have successfully added an extension to your Chrome browser!

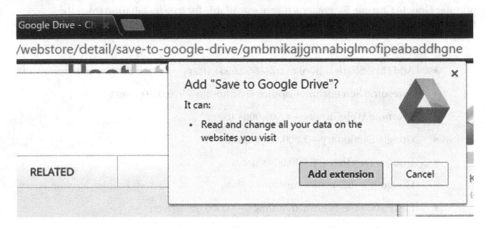

Figure 1-5. *Adding an extension from the store: confirming the selection*

As mentioned earlier, you can tab over to the URL chrome://extensions to see the list of added extensions. The extension just added will be available in that list (see Figure 1-6).

Figure 1-6. *Adding an extension from the store: Save to Google Drive*

■ **Note** Similar to the chrome-plugins-url (chrome://plugins) and the chrome-extensions-url (chrome://extensions), there are other useful URLs (Figure 1-7) that you can access to get more detailed information about your Chrome browser. To get a complete list of these URLs, open the page chrome://chrome-urls in your Chrome browser, as displayed in Figure 1-7.

List of Chrome URLs

- chrome://accessibility
- chrome://appcache-internals
- chrome://apps
- chrome://blob-internals
- chrome://bookmarks
- chrome://cache
- chrome://chrome
- chrome://chrome-urls
- chrome://components
- chrome://conflicts
- chrome://copresence
- chrome://crashes
- chrome://credits
- chrome://device-log
- chrome://devices
- chrome://discards
- chrome://dns
- chrome://downloads
- chrome://extensions
- chrome://flags

Figure 1-7. Chrome URLs at chrome://chrome-urls

Technologies to Create Extensions

While Google Chrome Extensions offer a lot to the users (in terms of the rich functionalities provided), at the same time they also provide a great ease to the developers in creating extensions. The technologies used to create Google Chrome Extensions are nothing but vanilla HTML, CSS, JavaScript, and (most essentially) JSON! And because of this, developing extensions for the Google Chrome browser has a flatter learning curve compared to developing extensions for other browsers. And yes, Google Chrome Extensions can be built from any desktop operating system. After all, these extensions are just a bunch of HTML and JavaScript files!

How Are Technologies Used?

For obvious reasons, HTML and CSS are used to create the views in extensions. JavaScript is used to provide the application logic, as well as to access the APIs and components provided by the Google Chrome Extensions framework (in-depth coverage of extension components and APIs is provided in Chapters 2 and 3, respectively). Finally, JSON is used to create the manifest file for the extensions, in order to provide information about itself (the extension) to the Google Chrome browser.

Extensions API

Google Chrome Extensions are sandboxed in Chrome browsers. This sandbox allows an *isolated* execution of the code (i.e., the JavaScript code) belonging to the extension. What this basically means is that there could be hundreds of extensions installed on the Chrome browser, but those extensions won't be aware of each other's existence automatically. And what this implies is:

- Different extensions won't accidentally connect with each other.
  - An extension cannot automatically access code or memory belonging to another extension.
- There won't be any name conflicts.
  - Chrome browser won't get confused between your extension's Script_A.js and another extension's Script_A.js.
  - The same holds true for other resources that belong to an extension, such as HTML, JSON files, images, etc.
- Extensions can connect with each other in a determined, controlled way (for communication).
  - The Extensions framework provides a messaging API to help with one-time as well as long-lived connections (more about it in Chapter 3).

> ■ **Note** Apart from the sandboxing described here, there is another kind of sandboxing that's provided by the Chrome browser (sandboxing of scripts that are injected from extensions into web pages). You will read about it in Chapter 3.

Chrome Extensions are extremely viable in enhancing the functionality of the Chrome web browser. They are able to do so by combining different features (of the Chrome browser) to provide a common functionality. For example, consider an extension that accesses the tabs and the alarms API (provided by Chrome) to open a tab after a predefined interval (say, one day).

The Google Chrome Extensions framework provides extensions with many special-purpose APIs that provide access to amazing features of the Chrome browser. These APIs provide access to almost every feature available in the Chrome browser!

> ■ **Note** While the Extensions framework provides a whole lot of special-purpose APIs, extensions can still use all the standard APIs (also known as the standard JavaScript APIs) that the browser provides to web pages. These are the same core JavaScript and Document Object Model (DOM) APIs that you are already familiar with. Additionally, XMLHttpRequest, HTML5 (and other emerging) APIs, WebKit APIs (for CSS animations, filters, etc.), and V8 APIs (such as JSON) are also supported!
>
> The HTML5 and other emerging APIs supported by the Chrome browser include audio, canvas, geolocation, local storage, notifications, and video. To read more about these APIs, visit the URL https://developer.chrome.com/extensions/api_other.

Using these APIs, you can integrate different features provided by the Chrome browser with our extension. The list of features includes APIs for alarms, bookmarks, history, tabs, actions, storage, notifications, search, and a lot more! You will learn about these APIs in Chapter 3.

Creating Your First Extension

The first extension that you will be creating is called ShowTime. This extension will add a clickable button (also known as the Browser-Action button) to the Google Chrome toolbar. Clicking this button will open a popup (see Figure 1-8) that will display the current time and date.

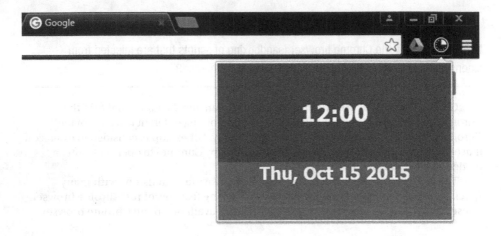

Figure 1-8. Extension popup displayed upon clicking the Extension button

---

■ **Note**   manifest.json is the only reserved file name in an extension. All the other files can be named anything you want.

To start off, you need to create a folder with the following files: popup.html, popup_script.js, icon.png, and manifest.json (see Figure 1-9).

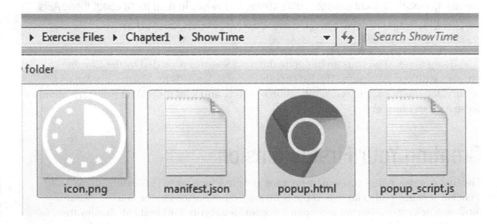

Figure 1-9. Exercise files: ShowTime

Later, when you learn about publishing, you will find that the same folder (that you just created) is zipped and uploaded to the Chrome Web Store.

■ **Note** A zipped package of the same folder will be uploaded on the Chrome Web Store (via the *Developer Dashboard*) when you publish this extension. This is also demonstrated in Figures 1-30 to 1-32. The same holds true for every extension you develop.

As described earlier, the HTML file represents the view our extension's popup will have. The JavaScript file will contain the application logic (in this case, logic to display the current time and date). The manifest file will provide information about the extension itself to the Chrome browser. For obvious reasons, the icon.png file will be used by the Chrome browser to create the button for your extension (see Figure 1-10).

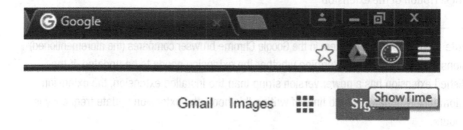

Figure 1-10. *Extension button in the Google Chrome toolbar*

Validating a JSON File

Now it's time to open the manifest.json file in your favorite text editor. But before you do, an important thing to note is that a JSON file *cannot* have comments inside it. This includes single-line and multi-line comments. Most errors during uploading of extension packages on the Chrome Web Store are caused due to such comments in the manifest file. These errors are not reported when testing extensions locally in the Chrome browser.

■ **Note** For the purpose of demonstration, however, *comments* have been used in the code listings and related material.

So, whenever you get a feeling that your manifest file is not in its best condition (i.e., it might contain some typos or other formatting errors), feel free to try out any *JSON validators* of your choice. There are tons of such validators available online. For example, http://jsonlint.com, http://jsonschemalint.com, etc. With that said, you can finally open the manifest file for editing.

Creating the Manifest

Add the following attributes to your empty manifest file: `manifest_version`, `name`, and `version`. These are the required fields in a manifest file. `manifest_version` represents the version of the manifest file format. `name` represents the name of the extension. And similarly, `version` is the version of the extension.

The `manifest_version` attribute takes an integer value greater than 0. At the time of writing, the valid value for the `manifest_version` attribute is 2, which indicates that it is the second version of the manifest file format. The `version` attribute takes a string value consisting of (one to four) dot-separated integers (between 0 and 65536). Similarly, the name attribute takes a string value containing the name of your extension. You can also add a `description` attribute (with a corresponding string value), which represents a plain text description of the extension.

■ **Note**   The auto-update system in the Google Chrome browser compares (the aforementioned) versions of an extension to determine whether the extension needs to be updated. If the published extension has a newer version string than the installed extension, the extension is automatically updated. At the time of writing this book, the extension update frequency is five hours.

Adding the Button: Browser-Action

Now you need to add the code for the clickable button in the Google Chrome toolbar. This is also known as the *Browser-Action* button, or simply Browser-Action. For this, you need to add another attribute in your manifest called `browser_action`. The `browser_action` attribute takes an object value (i.e. `{}`) comprised of the following (string) keys: `default_title`, `default_icon`, and `default_popup`.

As you can see in Listing 1-1, each of these keys take a string value. The `default_title` key represents the tooltip (string) for the Browser-Action. The `default_icon` key represents the (relative) path to the PNG image resource to be used as the icon. And similarly, `default_popup` represents the (relative) path to the HTML file to be used as the popup (view).

Listing 1-1. Chapter1/ShowTime/manifest.json

```
{
    "manifest_version" : 2,
    "name" : "ShowTime",
    "description" : "Extension to show the current time and date",
    "version" : "1.2",
    "browser_action" : {
        "default_title" : "ShowTime",
        "default_icon" : "icon.png", //Used as the icon in the Chrome toolbar
        "default_popup" : "popup.html"
    },
```

```
    "icons" : {
        "16" : "icon16.png", //Used as the favicon for an extension's pages
        "48" : "icon48.png", //Used on the extension management page
        "128" : "icon128.png" //Used during installation & in the Chrome Web Store
    }
}
```

Now you can move to the other parts, i.e., JavaScript and HTML code for the popup view. Not so surprisingly, creating the popup is no different from creating any other static web page. And regarding the JavaScript code, the Chrome Extensions framework while providing its special-purpose APIs, still provides all the standard JavaScript APIs.

It basically means that all the JavaScript code for the ShowTime extension can be written using standard JavaScript APIs. This includes the Date API (to get the current date and time),and the DOM API (to access the DOM tree).

You can try to create the JavaScript code for displaying the current time and date, say for example inside a heading tag (h1, h2, etc.). Listings 1-2 and 1-3 show one of the ways this can be done.

Listing 1-2. Chapter1/ShowTime/popup_script.js

```
//region {variables and functions}
var timeId = "time";
var dateId = "date";
var days = ["Sun","Mon","Tue","Wed","Thu","Fri","Sat"];
var months = ["Jan","Feb","Mar","Apr","May","Jun","Jul","Aug","Sep","Oct","
            Nov","Dec"];
var consoleGreeting = "Hello World! - from popup_script.js";
function setTimeAndDate(timeElement,dateElement) {
    var date = new Date();
    var minutes = (date.getMinutes() < 10 ? '0' : '') + date.getMinutes();
    var time = date.getHours() + ":" + minutes;
    //In "date.getMonth", 0 indicates the first month of the year
    //In "date.getDay", 0 represents Sunday
    var date = days[date.getDay()] + ", " + months[date.getMonth()] + "
    " + date.getDate() + " " + date.getFullYear();
    timeElement.innerHTML = time;
    dateElement.innerHTML = date;
}
//end-region
```

An important point to note in Listing 1-2 is that the getMonth method (of the Date object) returns 0 for the first month of the year. And the getDay method (of the Date object) returns 0 for Sunday. Also, the setTimeAndDate function takes two arguments. These arguments represent the elements used to display the current time and date.

Listing 1-3. Chapter1/ShowTime/popup_script.js

```
//region {calls}
console.log(consoleGreeting);
document.addEventListener("DOMContentLoaded",function(dcle) {
        var timeElement = document.getElementById(timeId);
        var dateElement = document.getElementById(dateId);
        setTimeAndDate(timeElement,dateElement);
});
//end-region
```

Listing 1-3 contains the remaining JavaScript code where the setTimeAndDate function is called. As displayed, it is a good practice to access the DOM after the document has loaded (which is why the setTimeAndDate function is called inside the listener for the DOMContentLoaded event).

You might be wondering about the output of the console.log method. This is discussed in one of the following topics on debugging extensions. But before that, you will first need to know how to load an extension in the browser. This is discussed in the next section, "Loading the Extension Folder".

Listing 1-4. Chapter1/ShowTime/popup.html

```
<!DOCTYPE html>
<html>
<head>

<!-- The following tag is not obeyed -->

<title>ShowTime (Custom)</title>

<!--
<script>
// Inline scripts are not allowed
alert('Hello World');
</script>
-->

<!-- Referring scripts is allowed -->

<script src="popup_script.js"></script>

<style>
body {
    padding:0px;
    margin:0px;
    width:300px;
    height:200px;
}
```

Take a look at Listings 1-4 and 1-5, which contain the HTML code. There is a very important point to note here. Inlining of scripts is *not allowed* in the popup! But scripts can be referred, as displayed in the code. The src should always point to the *relative* path to the script file (i.e. relative to the extension folder). Additionally, you can also split the application logic into multiple JavaScript files. But each should be referred separately. The CSS inside the style tag can also be extracted into an external CSS file and referred as `<link type="text/css" rel="stylesheet" href="some_file.css" />`.

Listing 1-5. Chapter1/ShowTime/popup.html

```
h1,h2 {
    display:table-row;
    vertical-align:middle;
    text-align:center;
}
h2 {
    background-color:#777;
}
.unselectable {
    -webkit-user-select:none;
    cursor:default;
}
</style>
</head>
<body>
    <div class="unselectable">
        <h1 class="empty"></h1>
        <h1 id="time"></h1>
        <h2 id="date"></h2>
    </div>
</body>
</html>
```

Loading the Extension Folder

The Chrome browser provides a very quick and easy way to load the extension folder in the browser (for testing purposes). Note that no additional file is required by the browser. It only expects to find a folder with HTML, JavaScript, and a JSON file. The following steps demonstrate how to load the extension folder:

1. Tab over to the Extensions Management page. Recall that this page is located at the URL chrome://extensions (Figure 1-1).

2. Turn on the Developer Mode option (seen in Figure 1-11) on this page.

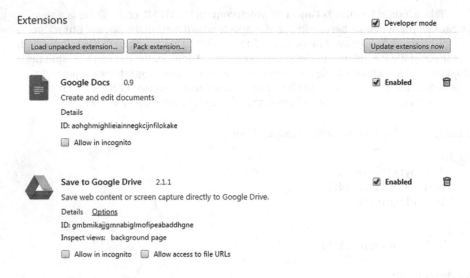

Figure 1-11. *Loading an extension: Choosing the developer mode option*

3. This will add an additional section to the page, with buttons to load, pack, and update extensions (as displayed in Figure 1-11).

4. Click on the Load Unpacked Extension button to load the extension. As displayed in Figure 1-12, a Browse for Folder or a similar window will prompt you to choose the extension folder.

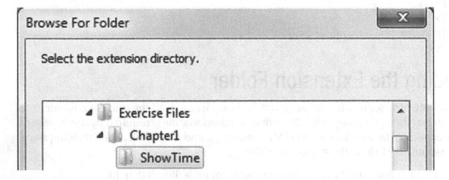

Figure 1-12. *Loading an extension: Browsing for the extension folder*

5. Select the ShowTime folder you created, and click OK to proceed. There it is! You have finally loaded your extension in the browser (see Figures 1-13 and 1-14). As discussed earlier, if your manifest file is malformed, an error will be shown at this stage ("Manifest is not valid JSON"). It will ask you to correct it and retry the loading process.

■ **Note** You can also enable the extension to run in the *incognito mode* by selecting the Allow in Incognito option from the Extensions Management page (see Figure 1-13).

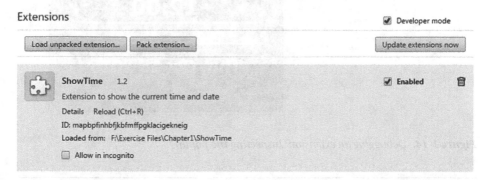

Figure 1-13. Loading an extension: Extension is listed in the Extensions Management page

As soon as the extension is successfully loaded, it will also be available (for configuration) in the Extensions Management page, as displayed in Figure 1-13. Finally, to view the popup, you need to click on the Browser-Action (button) corresponding to the ShowTime extension. Upon hovering over this button, you can also see the tooltip for the Browser-Action (recall that the tooltip string was set using the default_title key in the manifest file). Next, you'll find out how to debug Chrome Extensions.

Debugging an Extension

In this section, you learn about debugging Chrome Extensions. Not so surprisingly, this debugging is not different from debugging simple web pages on the Chrome browser. Your best friend for this task is—you guessed it—Chrome DevTools.

We won't be getting into great detail about Chrome DevTools, because the Google developers community has already provided excellent resources to get newbies, as well as experienced web developers, familiar with debugging web applications on the Chrome browser. The following URL will get you there: https://developers.google.com/web/tools/chrome-devtools/.

Inspecting the Popup

The first kind of debugging you can do is inspect the popup. To do that, simply right-click on the popup (after the popup gets displayed upon clicking the Browser-Action) and choose Inspect Element, as shown in Figure 1-14.

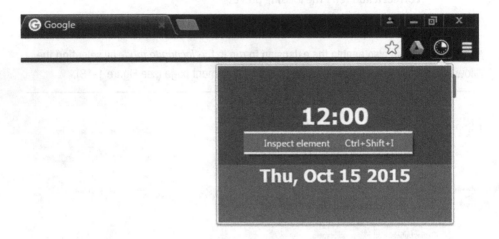

Figure 1-14. *Debugging an extension: Inspecting the popup*

■ **Note**   Alternatively, popups can also be inspected by selecting the Inspect Popup menu item, which is displayed when you right-click on the icon for the extension (i.e., the Browser-Action).

As displayed in Figure 1-15, the Chrome DevTools window will appear, with the Elements panel selected. You can use this panel to edit the styles, or even the DOM, in an iterative manner to see what's working best with your designs.

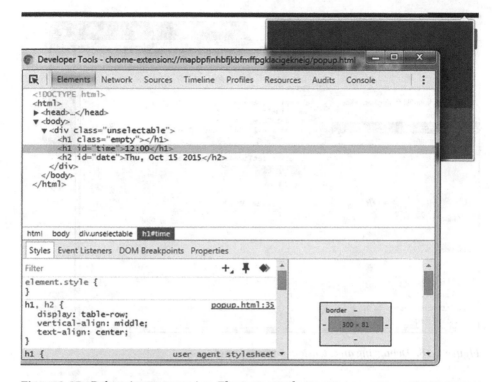

Figure 1-15. Debugging an extension: Elements panel

Sources and Resources Panel

The other panels that can be useful during debugging include the Sources panel and the Resources panel. Using the Sources panel, you can debug the JavaScript code by setting *breakpoints* in the script. In order to do that, you first need to select the particular script (see Figure 1-16) that needs to be debugged. Next, click the line number of the line where you want to set the breakpoint. Finally (while staying inside the DevTools window), reload the DevTools window to activate the breakpoint(s).

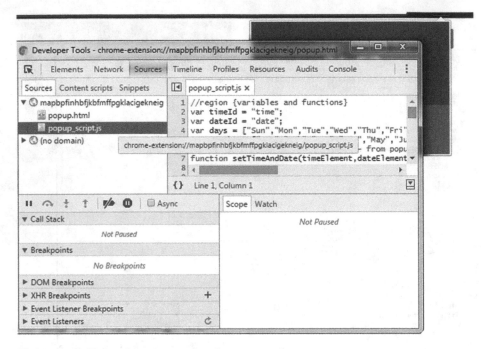

Figure 1-16. *Debugging an extension: Sources panel*

■ **Note**   You can also add multiple breakpoints to scripts in the Sources panel by clicking each line's line number.

Using the Resources panel, you can inspect the other resources that are loaded, such as local storage and session storage. We won't, however, use these kinds of storage for the purposes of this book, as the Google Chrome Extensions framework provides a better storage API for the extensions. It which allows syncing of the stored data across multiple devices, which is not provided by the localStorage and sessionStorage APIs.

You can still experiment with their use in the extensions you develop. Inspecting the storage via the Resources panel is extremely easy. As displayed in Figure 1-17, all you need to do is simply select the resource item with the kind of storage you need to inspect.

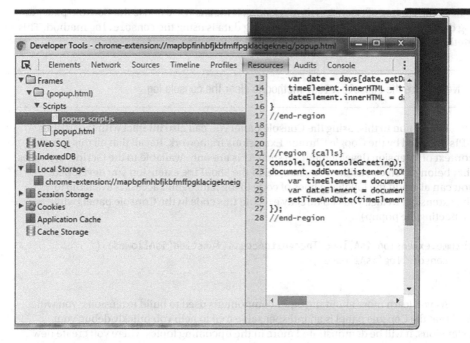

Figure 1-17. Debugging an extension: Resources panel

Console Panel

The Console panel is a typical (JavaScript) REPL in the Chrome DevTools window. Using it, not only can you log diagnostic information, you can also use it as a shell to interact with the JavaScript on the page. The Console panel is displayed in Figure 1-18.

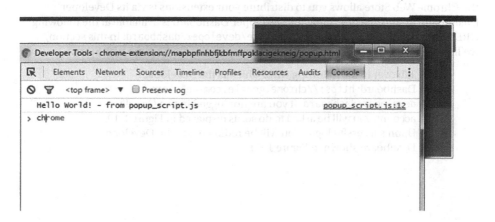

Figure 1-18. Debugging an extension: Console panel

In the context of extension development, it means you can use the Console panel to log data from the scripts. The way you can log data is using the `console.log` method. This method takes a variable list of JavaScript objects to output.

■ **Note**   Use the `console.clear` method to clear the console log.

In addition to this, using the Console panel you can also interact with the various APIs provided by the Google Chrome Extensions framework. Recall that all this is in the context of extension development, so such APIs are only available to the (scripts or) pages that belong to an extension. For example, in the ShowTime extension you developed, you can also add the following lines of code to log if incognito access is available to the extension. In fact, you can directly execute this code in the Console panel (while inspecting the popup).

```
chrome.extension.isAllowedIncognitoAccess(function(isAllowed) {
    console.log(isAllowed);
});
```

As you learn more about the other components used to build extensions, you will find that the Console panel is an indispensable tool to help you quickly debug your extensions. It will be demonstrated more in the upcoming topics where you create new extensions. For now, let's explore how to distribute extensions via the Chrome Web Store.

Distributing on Store

Once you create your awesome extension, you will soon find the need to distribute it on the Chrome Web Store. This will help you market your app, extension, or theme to a multitude of users in search of such products for their Chrome browsers. The way the Chrome Web Store allows you to distribute your extensions is via its Developer Dashboard. At the time of writing, the Developer Dashboard is available at the following URL: `https://chrome.google.com/webstore/developer/dashboard`. In this section, we'll go step by step to upload the ShowTime extension to the Chrome Web Store.

1. Tab over to the following URL, which is the Developer Dashboard: `https://chrome.google.com/webstore/developer/dashboard`. If you are not logged in to a Google account, you will be asked to do so, as displayed in Figure 1-19. Upon successful login, you will be redirected to the Developer Dashboard shown in Figure 1-20.

google.com/ServiceLogin?service=chromewebstore&continue=https://chrome.google.com/webstore/

Google

One account. All of Google.

Sign in to continue to Chrome Web Store

Prateek Mehta

Password

Sign in

Figure 1-19. *Distributing an extension: Logging into a Google account*

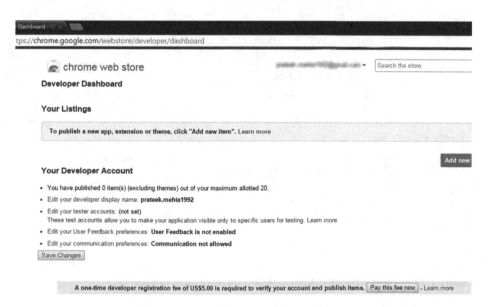

tps://**chrome.google.com**/webstore/developer/dashboard

chrome web store   Search the store

Developer Dashboard

Your Listings

To publish a new app, extension or theme, click "Add new item". Learn more

Add new

Your Developer Account

- You have published 0 item(s) (excluding themes) out of your maximum allotted 20.
- Edit your developer display name: **prateek.mehta1992**
- Edit your tester accounts: **(not set)**
  These test accounts allow you to make your application visible only to specific users for testing. Learn more
- Edit your User Feedback preferences: **User Feedback is not enabled**
- Edit your communication preferences: **Communication not allowed**

Save Changes

A one-time developer registration fee of US$5.00 is required to verify your account and publish items. Pay this fee now - Learn more

Figure 1-20. *Distributing an extension: Using the dashboard*

23

■ **Note** The Google Account ID does not necessarily have to be a Gmail ID, but commonly, it is.

2.   Once you are in the Developer Dashboard, you need to review the basic information about your developer account. At the time of writing, this information can be reviewed before paying the developer's registration fee.

■ **Note** A one-time developer registration fee of U.S. $5.00 is required to verify your account and publish items.

3.   Next, you need to pay the developer registration fee. It is a one-time fee, required to verify your account and publish items. At the time of writing, it amounts to U.S. $5.00. Click Pay This Fee Now button to initiate the payment process.

4.   As displayed in Figures 1-21 and 1-22, you need to add a payment method to pay with. If you already have a payment method associated with your Google account, you can proceed to the next step.

Figure 1-21. *Distributing an extension: Selecting a payment method*

Figure 1-22. *Distributing an extension: Adding a new payment method*

5. Review your purchase (see Figure 1-23) and then click Buy to proceed to the next step.

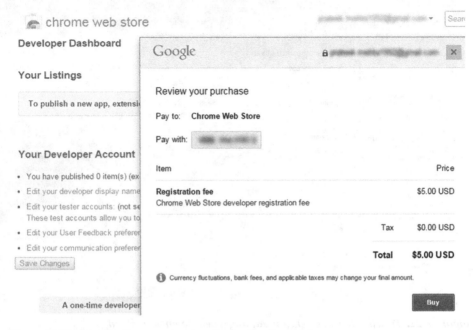

Figure 1-23. *Distributing an extension: Reviewing the purchase*

6. Finally, you can start the payment gateway by clicking the Start Now button, shown in Figure 1-24.

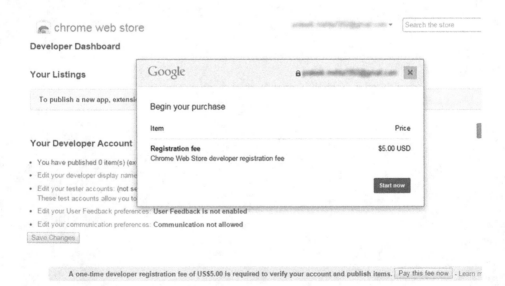

Figure 1-24. *Distributing an extension: Confirming the purchase*

7. Upon successful completion of the payment process, a window will be displayed from *Google Wallet*, thanking you for the purchase. As displayed in Figure 1-25, click Done to return to the Developer Dashboard.

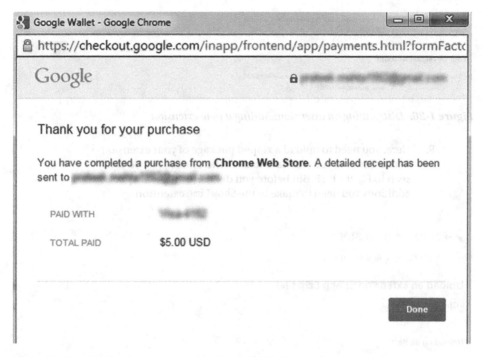

Figure 1-25. *Distributing an extension: Completing the purchase*

■ **Note**   Currency fluctuations, bank fees, and applicable taxes may change your final amount.

---

8. In the Developer Dashboard, click the Add New Item button (see Figure 1-26) to upload a new extension to your dashboard.

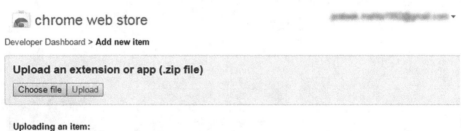

Figure 1-26. *Distributing an extension: Adding a new extension*

9. Here, you need to upload a zipped package of your extension folder. For that, you will have to click the Choose File button seen in Figure 1-27. But before you do, there are some quick additions you need to make to the ShowTime extension.

chrome web store

Developer Dashboard > **Add new item**

Upload an extension or app (.zip file)

Choose file | Upload

Uploading an item:

- Upload a ZIP file of your item directory, not a packaged CRX file.
- Include a well-designed product icon in your manifest (more info).
- Read the documentation about creating and packaging apps.
- Need more help? Check out the Chrome Web Store developer documentation.

Figure 1-27. *Distributing an extension: Uploading the zipped package*

10. As shown in Listing 1-1, you need to add the icons attribute to the manifest file. This attribute takes an object value (i.e. {}) of the following key-value pairs:

a. "16" : "icon16.png": This 16px icon is used as the favicon for an extension's pages

b. "48" : "icon48.png": This 48px icon is used on the Extensions Management page (as displayed in Figure 1-28)

c. "128" : "icon128.png": This 128px icon is used during installation and in the Chrome Web Store

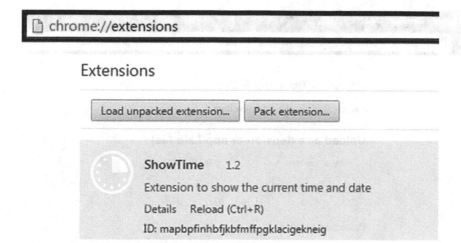

Figure 1-28. *Distributing an extension: 48px icon*

11. Now that you have added the icons attribute to the manifest,
     you also need to add the corresponding images. You can
     create your own or use the ones provided in the Exercise
     Files folder for Chapter 1 (see Figure 1-29). Note that the keys
     16, 48, and 128 represent the (relative) paths to the PNG image
     resources to be used.

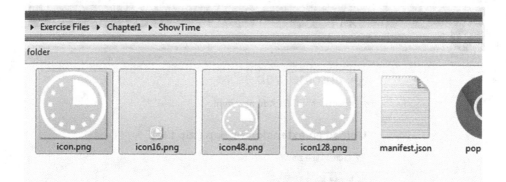

Figure 1-29. *Distributing an extension: Adding the icons*

12. Finally, you can create a zipped package of this extension
     folder and resume from Step 9.

13. After choosing the zipped package, click the Upload button
     (see Figure 1-30).

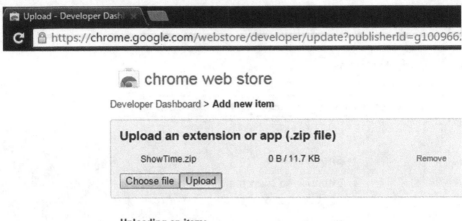

Figure 1-30. *Distributing an extension: Uploading the ShowTime zipped package*

14. Upon successful uploading of the zipped package, the
dashboard will reload (see Figure 1-31) to reflect the changes.

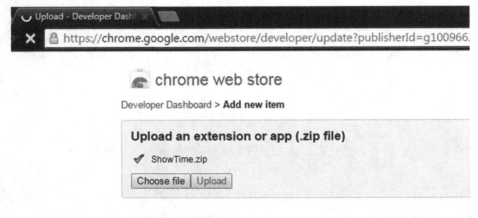

Figure 1-31. *Distributing an extension: Uploading the ShowTime zipped package*

15. If your manifest file is malformed (or there are any other related flaws, for example missing image resources, etc.), an error will be shown at this stage, as displayed in Figure 1-32.

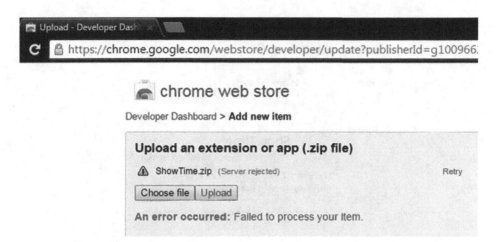

Figure 1-32. Distributing an extension: Uploading the ShowTime zipped package

16. You then enter the edit mode for your extension (see Figure 1-33). You are free to fill in the fields the way you want.

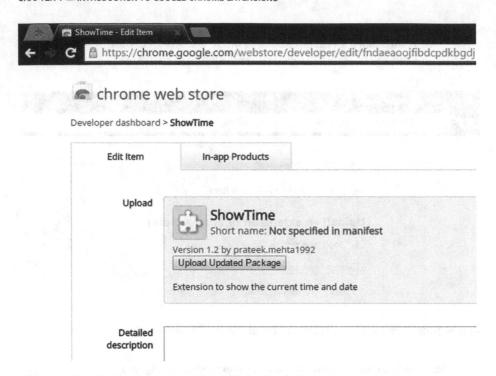

Figure 1-33. *Distributing an extension: Editing the draft*

17. Finally, you can either publish the changes you made, which will also publish the extension on the store, or you can choose to save the draft. You may also discard the current draft if you want to try again. For now, save the draft by clicking on Save Draft and Return to Dashboard, as displayed in Figure 1-34.

Requirements	No requirements
Visibility options	● Public Everyone can see it ○ Unlisted Only people with the link can see it. ○ Private Only trusted testers from your developer dashboard can see it. You can also include members of a Google Group that you own or manage.

Discard draft | Save draft and return to dashboard   Preview changes | Publish changes

Figure 1-34. *Distributing an extension: Saving the draft*

When you return to the dashboard, you will find the draft of your extension listed under the Your Listings section, as displayed in Figure 1-35. As you learn more about the development of extensions, you can improve and update this draft. And finally, when you are ready with this extension, you can update the fields discussed in Step 16 and publish the extension.

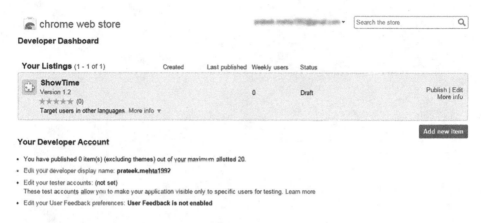

Figure 1-35. Distributing an extension: Item listings

Summary

This chapter began with a basic definition of browser extensions, including what they are and what they are not. Then you learned to list the extensions installed in your Chrome browser via the Extensions Management page.

Next, some notable extensions were discussed, after which you also learned to install extensions on the Chrome browser. The technologies to create Chrome Extensions were also described, while comparing them with the technologies used on other browsers.

Finally you created your first extension—called ShowTime—and you learned to load it in the Chrome browser. Not only this, you also learned to debug your extension and upload it on the Chrome Web Store. In Chapter 2, you will read more about the development of Chrome Extensions, as well as their architecture. But before moving ahead, make sure to fiddle and experiment with things in the ShowTime extension you created to get a better feel of the development process. This will make you more comfortable with the sample extensions that are used in the next chapter, where you learn about the architecture of extensions.

CHAPTER 2

■ ■ ■

Architecture Overview

This chapter describes the architecture of Chrome Extensions from the user's and developer's points of view. Doing so will help you quickly wrap your head around various components that are used to create Chrome Extensions. After reading this chapter, you will understand the building blocks of Chrome Extensions like a user—in terms of the interactive functionalities involved—and also like a developer—in terms of the inner techniques available to provide various functionalities.

Like the previous chapter, this chapter assumes you have some experience writing simple web pages using technologies such as HTML, CSS, and JavaScript. You should know the event-driven nature of web pages, for example—showing some UI after clicking a button (using event listeners), etc. That said, let's begin!

What Is User Perspective?

An API (in our case, the Google Chrome Extensions API) can be understood in terms of the inner techniques involved in providing various functionalities (such as UI, storage, etc.) or in terms of the interactive functionalities—down to the techniques that need to be used to access these functionalities. The latter—i.e., understanding the Extension's API in terms of the *interactive functionalities* it provides—is described as the user perspective (or the user's point of view). The contents of this chapter switch perspective from time to time, to aid your learning of the Google Chrome Extensions API.

Components Involved in Creating Chrome Extensions

Google Chrome Extensions are no different from any other software application. You interact with it via inputs such as buttons (or shortcut keys, etc.), and it processes some data and displays the result. Abstract, isn't it? Well, not so much. You will find out soon.

Similar to other application development frameworks, the Google Chrome Extensions framework provides its developers with techniques to provide UI, and functionalities such as storage, messaging, web requests, etc. The following are the components that are used to create Chrome Extensions.

© Prateek Mehta 2016
P. Mehta, *Creating Google Chrome Extensions*, DOI 10.1007/978-1-4842-1775-7_2

- **Input components**—Offer interactive functionalities, comprised of UI/non-UI input elements, such as toolbar buttons, shortcut keys, context menu items, etc. Chrome Extensions provide the following input components (see Figure 2-1):

  - Browser-Action

  - Page-Action

  - Shortcut-Key

  - Context-Menu-Item

  - Omnibox-Input

  - Content-UI

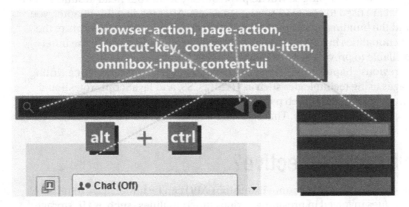

Figure 2-1. Input components for creating Chrome Extensions

- **Scripting components**—As the name suggests, these components are scripts that contain the application logic which may be required at different times when users interact with the extension. There are three types of scripting components:

  - *Event scripts (Background scripts)*

  - *Popup scripts*

  - *Content scripts*

■ **Note** Each *type* of scripting component has its own separate *scope*. So, for example, a popup script cannot use variables and functions defined in an event script, and vice versa. The same holds true for other pairs of scripts—content scripts and popup scripts, and content scripts and event script. The only way scripts can access each other's data (variables, functions, etc.) is by *messaging*, which you will learn about in the next chapter.

- **Popup component**—Popup is a special (optional) view
  available only to the Browser-Action and Page-Action input
  components. A popup is made entirely of an HTML page
  (see Figures 2-2 and 2-3). Note that a popup *only* appears
  when the user clicks on the toolbar button corresponding
  to a Browser-Action or a Page-Action (whichever one the
  extension is using). And yes, you guessed it right—popup
  scripts are used along with the popup component.

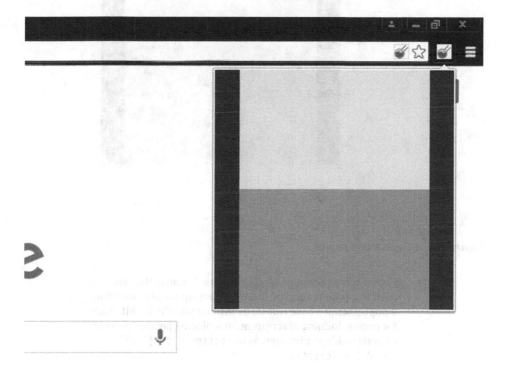

Figure 2-2. *A Browser-Action popup*

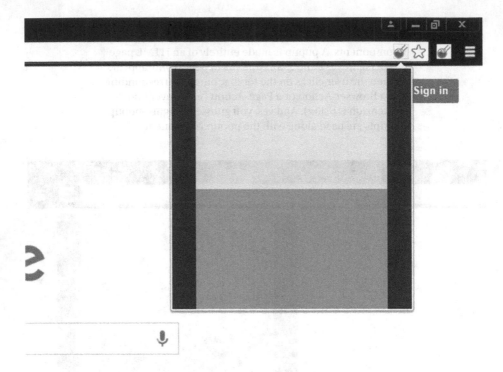

Figure 2-3. *A Page-Action popup*

- Popup scripts are plain JavaScript files. Because they are used in a popup, they are known as popup scripts. Note that a popup script's code *cannot* be inlined into the HTML page for popup. Inlining of scripts means placing JavaScript code directly inside script tags, as in <script>alert('Hello World');</script>.

- So, popup scripts can only be referred to, where the src needs to point a path, relative to the extension folder, such as <script src="popup_script.js"></script>. And yes, multiple popup scripts can be referred to (see Listing 2-1) to modularize the code. These scripts do not get merged when the extension loads (in the browser), and they can be separately identified in the Sources and Resources panels (see Figures 1-16 and 1-17 in Chapter 1) in the DevTools window, discussed in Chapter 1. Additionally, the Console panel will also help categorize the logs from different (referred) popup scripts, as displayed in Figure 2-4.

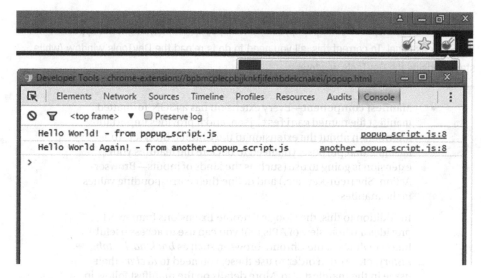

Figure 2-4. Inspecting the popup: Console panel

- A very important feature of popup scripts is that they can access the Chrome Extensions API. Moreover, being JavaScript files, popup scripts have access to all the Standard JavaScript APIs, including the event APIs to listen for and respond to DOM events fired from the nodes within a popup.

Listing 2-1. Chapter2/HelloBrowserAction/popup.html

```
<head>

<!-- The following tag is not obeyed -->
<title>HelloBrowserAction (Custom)</title>

<!--
<script>
// Inline scripts are not allowed
alert('Hello World');
</script>
-->

<!-- Referring scripts is allowed -->
<script src="popup_script.js"></script>
<script src="another_popup_script.js"></script>

<style>

...
```

■ **Note**   While inspecting the popup, sometimes, popup script(s) might not appear in the Sources panel. To correct this, all you need to do is reload the DevTools window (while staying inside the DevTools window).

- **Manifest component**—Every extension has a JSON-formatted manifest file named `manifest.json`, and it provides important information about the extension to the Chrome browser. To facilitate that purpose, you need to declare the features your extension is going to use (such as the kinds of inputs—Browser-Action, Shortcut-Key, etc.) and define their corresponding values in the manifest.

  In addition to this, the Google Chrome Extensions framework provides a whole slew of APIs that you can use to access useful functionalities of the Chrome browser, such as *bookmarks*, *tabs*, *history*, etc. And in order to use these, you need to *declare* their usage in the manifest also. More details on the manifest follow in the upcoming topics in this chapter.

  At the time of writing this book, to create the simplest valid Google Chrome Extension (that does nothing), the only requirement is a folder with a manifest file that contains the following required attributes (also discussed in Chapter 1).

  - `manifest_version`—Indicates the version of the manifest file format (at the time of writing, it is 2)

  - `name` —Indicates the name of the extension, for example `HelloBrowserAction`

  - `version`—Indicates the version of the extension, for example `1.2`

Extension Runtime

In this section you learn about Extensions development from the developer's point of view. Specifically, you will learn about the *extension runtime* (not to be confused with the actual runtime API provided by the Extensions framework, i.e., the `chrome.runtime` API).

By now you understand that an extension's logic is written in JavaScript. And given the event-driven nature of JavaScript, you might be wondering about the extension lifecycle. For example, considering the various input components used to create extensions, you might wonder about listening to events fired from these inputs, and then responding accordingly.

Every input component in the Extensions framework (with the exception of Content-UI) has some associated events (for example, Browser-Action and Page-Action input components have the following events associated with them respectively—the `chrome.browserAction.onClicked` event and the `chrome.pageAction.onClicked` event). And to listen to these events, you need to attach *listener* functions. These functions are created (and assigned to events) within the scripting components that represent the extension runtime.

So, when an extension is loaded in the browser, the manifest is first read for providing permission(s) to access certain APIs (such as the *tabs* API). Then, the views and scripts get loaded. And finally, listener functions are assigned to input components. Note that the extension itself has some events associated with it (for example, onMessage, onInstalled, etc.), and listener functions can also be assigned to these events by the scripting components that represent the extension runtime. Now, you may ask which scripting components represent the extension runtime. The following topic provides the answer to this question.

___

■ **Note**   The extension itself has many events associated with it. These events are properties of the chrome.runtime (API) object. Following are some of the most useful events associated with the extension—onMessage, onConnect, onConnectExternal, onInstalled, and onUpdateAvailable.

___

Scripts Representing the Runtime

In a loaded extension, the scripts (scripting components) that can listen for events fired from the input components, or other things that happen to an extension, represent the extension runtime. These scripts include the popup script and the event script. But because a popup script is only executed when a popup is opened, you will rely more on the event script in your extension (which is a long-running script in the background) to listen for each and every event (fired from any input component, or fired from the extension itself, including those that are fired when an extension installs, uninstalls, updates, etc.).

The script that does not represent the extension runtime is the content script. And obviously, the web pages loaded in the browser can never represent the extension runtime. But, as you will see in Chapter 3, web page scripts can still interact with the extension runtime and with the content scripts (using the messaging APIs).

___

■ **Note**   Content scripts (a type of scripting component that is injected into the visited web pages) have very limited access to the Chrome Extensions API, because they do not represent the extension runtime. They can only access the following APIs—chrome. runtime, chrome.extension, and chrome.storage. But content scripts have access to all the standard JavaScript APIs that regular web page scripts do. Additionally, they can interact with the extension runtime (using the messaging APIs).

___

Input Components: Part One

Input components are the *interactive functionalities* offered by the Google Chrome Extensions framework. Extensions do not heavily rely on inputs. But they are crucial, as these are the entry points to the extensions' core logic. For example, consider an extension that searches for a word in URLs from all opened tabs and returns matched URLs. For that it is required that the extension at least provide a toolbar button (i.e., a Browser-Action or Page-Action, as described next), which upon being pressed, displays a popup with text field to enter the word to be searched. Similar to this scenario, there are many other ways in which an extension will rely on one or more input components to trigger certain responses (from the scripting components) or to simply display the popup.

■ **Note** *Most* of these input components can be combined in a single extension. For example, the Google Dictionary (by Google) extension uses Browser-Action, Content-UI (where events are attached to document content), and Shortcut-Key as input components.

So, now you understand what inputs are. Let's learn more about them, including how are they used, and how to declare and define them in the manifest. Let me also reiterate that the manifest is the place where you declare the features your extension is going to use and define their corresponding values.

But before moving ahead, keep in mind that fully functional extensions can be created *without* any input components. For example, an extension that automatically sends the details of the visited web pages to an HTTP server. In addition to this example, *theme* that are created for the Chrome browser are also created without any input components. As a matter of fact, themes are solely created using a manifest component (and some images). Besides, a theme is an extension too! You learned to create themes in the last chapter.

The Browser-Action and Page-Action Components

The Browser-Action and Page-Action components are buttons in the Google Chrome toolbar, as displayed in Figure 2-1. Browser-Action is always located just right of the address bar (outside it), whereas Page-Action is always located inside the address bar (aligned to its right edge). In Figure 2-1, Browser-Action is the circular, purple button, just to the right of the omnibox. Page-Action is the triangular, light-purple button that's located inside the omnibox. Note that an extension can *only* use one of these—either a Browser-Action or a Page-Action component.

Both, Browser-Action and Page-Action have a *popup* component associated with them (along with an icon and a title). This popup gets displayed upon clicking on the icon corresponding to a Browser-Action or a Page-Action button. The title assigned in the manifest for these actions is set as the *tooltip* for the Browser-Action or Page-Action button (whichever one you are using). The Browser-Action and Page-Action APIs can be accessed from all the scripting components, except content scripts. The chrome. browserAction object is used to access the API for Browser-Action. Similarly, the chrome.pageAction object is used to access the API for Page-Action.

■ **Note**   In Google Chrome browser, the address bar is also known as an *omnibox*.
Throughout this book, these words are used interchangeably.

Need for Separate Actions

While a Browser-Action represents an action that is common to all web pages, it is not
so with a Page-Action. Page-Actions are meant for specific web pages (for example, web
pages belonging to facebook.com, web pages with password fields, etc.). This is why a
Page-Action is named so. This is a recommendation from Chrome, but there is nothing
to stop you from going against it. You could use Page-Actions for all web pages instead
of (the recommended way) only specific ones. But still, in terms of the API and the
architecture, there is a limitation set on Page-Actions that makes it quite clear what they
are actually intended for.

Once declared and defined in the manifest, a Browser-Action is always visible. This is
not so with a Page-Action. In order to display the Page-Action button in the browser, a call
to the chrome.pageAction.show(tabId) method needs to be made (see Listings 2-7 and
2-8) from any of the scripting components (except a content script). In addition to this,
the chrome.declarativeContent API can also be used to display Page-Actions (don't get
overwhelmed, as you will learn more about these APIs in the topics that follow).

■ **Note**   In the context of extensions development, every tab has a unique ID. Additionally,
in the Chrome Extensions framework, every tab is represented using the Tab type. This type
has many properties associated with it and important ones include id, active, and url.
The complete list of properties is available at the URL https://developer.chrome.com/
extensions/tabs#type. The chrome.tabs API is used to manipulate the tabs. You will read
more about this in the upcoming topics in this chapter.

Note that the popup component is available to Browser-Action and Page-Action
input components. And because a popup script is always attached to the popup, it is
implied that this script is always available to these input components (obviously, as
long as the popup is visible after the user clicks on these input components). The popup
component has the sole purpose of containing additional views, for example, form fields.
But to display a popup, the button corresponding to a Browser-Action or Page-Action
component needs to be clicked.

Role of the Manifest for This Component

The Browser-Action and Page-Action components need to be declared in the manifest
file. Apart from the declarations, you also need to define these components (whichever
one you are using in your extension). Browser-Action is declared (and defined) in the
following way (Listing 2-2) in the manifest file.

Listing 2-2. Chapter2/HelloBrowserAction/manifest.json

```
"browser_action" : {
    "default_title" : "HelloBrowserAction",
    "default_icon" : "icon.png",
    "default_popup" : "popup.html"
}
```

Similarly, Listing 2-3 displays how to declare (and define) a Page-Action in the manifest file. You are reminded again that *an extension can use only one of these*—either the Browser-Action or Page-Action component, but not both.

Listing 2-3. Chapter2/HelloPageAction/manifest.json

```
"page_action" : {
    "default_title" : "HelloPageAction",
    "default_icon" : "icon.png",
    "default_popup" : "popup.html"
}
```

As you can see, the declaration and definition go together for these two input components. Simply saving the manifest with only the attributes (browser_action or page_action) will produce errors when you try to upload this package into the Chrome browser for testing. So, along with the attribute, you also need to provide the corresponding value. For the Browser-Action and Page-Action components, those values are key-value pairs with the following keys.

- default_title—Set as the tooltip for the extension

- default_icon—PNG image resource at this path is set as the icon for the extension

- default_popup—HTML file at this path is set as the popup for the extension

---

■ **Note**   All resource paths provided in the manifest file are relative to the root of your extension folder. For example, if you have a folder named HelloWorldExtension that contains the manifest, then default-icon "icon.png" is taken relative to the root. It would be HelloWorldExtension/icon.png. So make sure you only provide relative paths.

Defining the Component

For the browser_action or page_action attributes, null, empty-string, bool, etc. are all invalid values. The only allowed value is an object, i.e. {}. This object can be left empty. This is usually done for quick deployment of an extension, for testing purposes. Moreover, sometimes you may want so intentionally for another reason (as explained ahead).

Whatever the scenario is, an extension will load successfully with an empty object as the value for a browser_action or page_action attribute.

You may be puzzled by how this works without providing the values. Well, it works because Chrome will provide a default extension icon (as seen in Figure 2-5) and a default title (using the name you have assigned to your extension in the manifest file for the name attribute). No default popup will be set for this action.

Figure 2-5. *Default extension icon in Google Chrome browser*

Note that all these attribute keys are prefixed with default because their values can be overridden by the extension runtime using certain API calls (provided by the Chrome Extensions framework). The calls are listed in Tables 2-1 and 2-2 for the Page-Action and Browser-Action components, respectively.

Table 2-1. *Page-Action: Setting Title, Icon, and Popup*

Method	Description
chrome.pageAction. setTitle(object details)	Details object takes keys tabId and title, where (integer) tabId is the ID of the tab for which you want to modify the Page-Action and title is the tooltip string.
chrome.pageAction. setIcon(object details, function callback)	Details object takes keys tabId and path, where path is the relative image path. The (optional) callback parameter should be a function that looks like function() {...}.
chrome.pageAction. setPopup(object details)	Details object takes keys tabId and popup, where popup is the HTML file to show in a popup. If it's set to the empty string (""), no popup is shown.

Table 2-2. *Browser-Action: Setting Title, Icon, and Popup*

Method	Description
chrome.browserAction. setTitle(object details)	Details object takes keys tabId and title, where (integer) tabId is the ID of the tab for which you want to limit this modification and title is the tooltip string. The tooltip is reset when this tab is closed.
chrome.browserAction. setIcon(object details, function callback)	Details object takes keys tabId and path, where path is the relative image path. The (optional) callback parameter should be a function that looks like function() {...}. The icon is reset when this tab is closed.
chrome.browserAction. setPopup(object details)	Details object takes keys tabId and popup, where popup is the HTML file to show in a popup. If it's set to the empty string (""), no popup is shown. The popup is reset when this tab is closed.

Component Usage

Now that you understand what these components are, let us discuss how we will be using them in the topic "Examples on Components" – which contains demo extensions for your learning purposes. As mentioned earlier, a Browser-Action component is used in an extension where a common functionality is desired for every visited page. An example of such an extension is a note-taking extension used to take notes on different pages.

You will be working with this note-taking extension in the topic "BrowserActionNotes" (to utilize a Browser-Action). And for the Page-Action demo, you'll be working with a modified version of the BrowserActionNotes extension, where note-taking will only be allowed on web pages belonging to the stackoverflow.com host. Additionally, the use of an event script to show Page-Actions has been demonstrated in the topic "HelloPageAction Extension".

Shortcut Key or Command

Shortcut key (or command) is another useful input component. As its name suggests, a shortcut key is a keyboard shortcut that can be registered as an input to your extension. Each such shortcut key must be listed in the manifest as an attribute of the commands manifest attribute, as seen in Listing 2-4. An extension can have many such shortcut key attributes, but there can only be a total of four keyboard shortcuts mapped to these attributes.

Listing 2-4. Chapter2/HelloShortcutKey/manifest.json

```json
{
    "manifest_version" : 2,
    "name" : "HelloShortcutKey",
    "description" : "Extension to demonstrate a Shortcut-Key as an input
    component",
    "version" : "1.2",
    "browser_action" : {
        "default_title" : "HelloShortcutKey",
        "default_icon" : "icon-1.png"
    },
    "background" : {
        "scripts" : ["event_script.js"],
        "persistent" : false
    },
    "commands" : {
        "shortcut-key to change the extension icon" : {
            "suggested_key" : {"default" : "Alt+Shift+9"},
            "description" : "Change the extension icon"
        }
    }
}
```

In Listing 2-4, only one shortcut key has been used. As mentioned, the shortcut key
(shortcut-key to change the extension icon) is listed as an attribute of the commands
manifest attribute. The actual keyboard shortcut that is mapped to the shortcut key is
defined as a value of the default attribute of the suggested_key attribute. It is named
default as it can be overridden.

The user can manually add more shortcuts from the chrome://extensions/
configureCommands window (see Figures 2-6 and 2-7). The API associated with the
shortcut key input component feature is accessible from the chrome.commands object. All
scripting components, except for content scripts, can use this API.

47

Figure 2-6. *Registering a shortcut for the HelloBrowserAction extension*

Figure 2-7. *A registered shortcut for the HelloBrowserAction extension*

In addition to this, attributes _execute_browser_action and _execute_page_action are reserved by Chrome for executing Browser-Action and Page-Action respectively. Command attributes should not have an _ as a prefix to their names because this will cause the commands API to fail silently.

Note that in Figures 2-6 and 2-7, only one attribute can be seen for the HelloBrowserAction extension. This attribute is generated by Chrome automatically. If you define your custom shortcuts, those will be visible in the chrome://extensions/configureCommands window, as shown for the HelloShortcutKey extension in Figure 2-8.

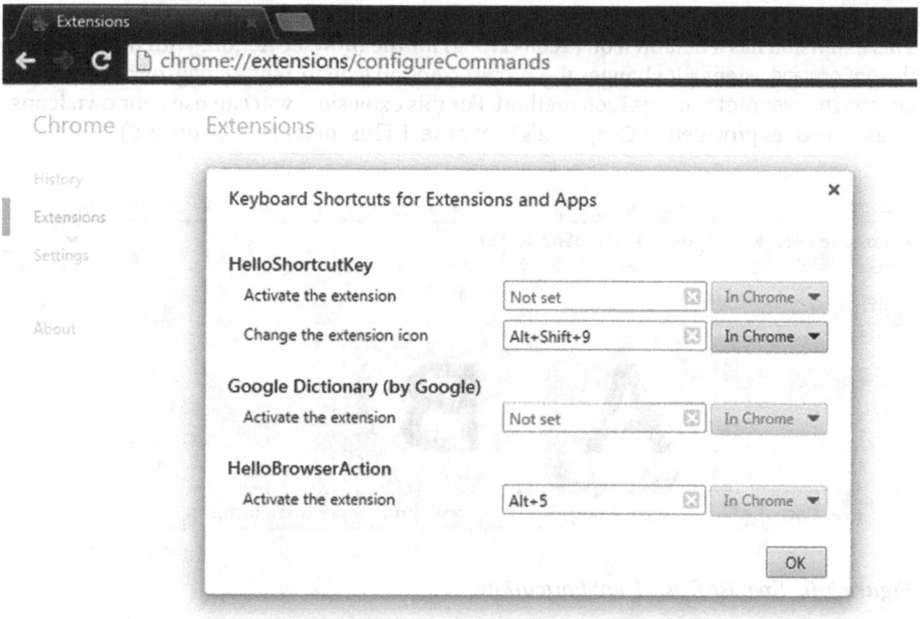

Figure 2-8. HelloShortcutKey extension with its custom shortcut key

The onCommand Event

Once you have defined a shortcut key for your extension, you can implement its
listener function by listening for the onCommand (`chrome.commands.onCommand`) event.
As discussed earlier, only the extension runtime (not to be confused with the `chrome.`
`runtime` API) can listen for such events. Specifically, the script that can do so is the event
script in an extension (refer back to the topic "Scripts Representing Runtime" to remind
yourself about the extension runtime).

Listing 2-5. Chapter2/HelloShortcutKey/event_script.js

```javascript
//region {variables and functions}
var consoleGreeting = "Hello World! - from event_script.js";
var details = {"path":"icon-2.png"};
//end-region

//region {calls}
console.log(consoleGreeting);
chrome.commands.onCommand.addListener(function(command) {
    chrome.browserAction.setIcon(
        details,
        function() {/**/}
    );
});
//end-region
```

Listings 2-4 and 2-5 contain the code sample from the HelloShortcutKey extension. This extension has a default icon (icon-1.png) for the Browser-Action. With the help of the onCommand listener, it changes the Browser-Action icon to icon-2.png, by calling the chrome.browserAction.setIcon method. For this extension, you can use your own icons or use the ones provided in Chapter 2's Exercise Files folder (see Figure 2-9).

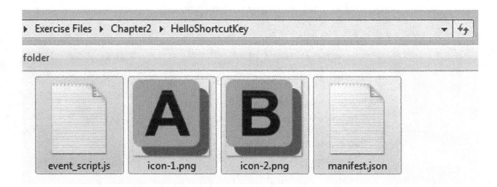

Figure 2-9. *Exercise files: HelloShortcutKey*

As seen in Listing 2-5, the addListener method is used to attach a listener to the onCommand event. The listener function receives a string argument "command", which represents name of the command (i.e., shortcut key) that was performed. In this case, if "command" is logged to the console, it will display the string "shortcut-key to change the extension icon". This argument is useful when an extension has multiple commands defined in the manifest. To separate the logic inside the listener (based on different commands) you need to branch out on different commands (names) that were performed (for example, using if or switch). Obviously, it's best to avoid the use of long and descriptive names for commands to make the comparisons easier.

■ **Note**   Do not get confused between the addListener and the addEventListener methods. The latter belongs to the DOM API, which you are already familiar with.

Event Scripts

In the previous topic, you learned about the event-script scripting component. Let's discuss more about this scripting component, including how it is declared in the manifest, why it needs to represent the extension runtime, and how persistent it is compared to other scripts.

> ■ **Note**   Popup scripts also represent the extension runtime. But they do not enjoy as many privileges (for example, persistence) as an event script (because a popup script is only executed when the corresponding popup is opened). So, there are only a few events which popup scripts can successfully listen to.

The Need for Event Scripts

Every component discussed so far has a specific purpose. For example, the Browser-Action and Page-Action components serve as button inputs; a shortcut key provides an alternative way of providing inputs; a popup component provides a view, and a popup script provides the application logic. Now you might have some rough idea as to how an event script is useful to an extension (based on your reading so far). The following points clearly define its uses:

- The most important use is listening for events fired from input components, such as click events fired from the Browser-Action or Page-Action components, command events when invoking a shortcut key, and context menu events from context menu item selection. Moreover, an event script can also listen for events fired from an omnibox input. Following is a complete list of events (fired from input components) along with the corresponding input component APIs (here, all input components are listed except for Content-UI).

  - `chrome.browserAction—onClicked`

  - `chrome.pageAction—onClicked`

  - `chrome.commands—onCommand`

  - `chrome.contextMenus—onClicked`

  - `chrome.omnibox—onInputStarted, onInputChanged, onInputEntered, onInputCancelled`

> ■ **Note**   The `onClicked` event will not fire if the Browser-Action or Page-Action component has `default_popup` defined in the manifest.

- Another important use is listening for events fired from the extension itself. This includes events such as `onMessage`, `onConnect`, `onInstalled`, `onUpdateAvailable`, etc., that are only accessible from the `chrome.runtime` object. Most of these events are part of the messaging API provided by the Chrome Extensions framework. You will read about these events in the next chapter.

■ **Note**   Content scripts (a type of scripting component that is injected into the visited web pages) can be used to create HTML elements in the host web pages. These elements are referred as Content UIs in this book. Content UIs can only fire standard JavaScript events.

Additionally, content scripts have very limited access to the Chrome Extensions API because they do not represent the extension runtime. They can only access the following APIs—`chrome.runtime`, `chrome.extension`, and `chrome.storage`. Content scripts can still communicate with the extension runtime using the messaging API (accessible via the `chrome.runtime` object) provided by the Chrome Extensions framework.

- As you will see in Chapter 3, using the `onMessage` (or `onConnect`) event, an event script can listen for messages from content scripts(s), injected into a web page by the extension. Additionally, using the `chrome.runtime.onMessageExternal` event, event scripts can also listen for messages directly from a web page.

- Apart from all these events, event scripts can also listen for events that are associated with various API features, such as `tabs`, `alarms`, `storage`, `bookmarks`, `history`, etc. Examples of such events (along with their corresponding APIs) are listed here:

  - `chrome.tabs`—`onCreated`, `onUpdated`, `onRemoved`, etc.

  - `chrome.alarms`—`onAlarm`

  - `chrome.storage`—`onChanged`

  - `chrome.bookmarks`—`onCreated`, `onRemoved`, `onChanged`, `onImportBegan`, `onImportEnded`, etc.

  - `chrome.history`—`onVisited`, `onVisitRemoved`

- Most important of all is the *persistence* of event-script, which gives rise to all of these features. An event script can listen for events in a reliable manner because it is a long-running script (unlike the popup script, which is only executed when the popup is opened). Event scripts are automatically loaded whenever they are *needed* (i.e., when the events they are listening to get fired) and are unloaded when they go idle again.

- Lastly, event scripts can also be used for containing the application logic that is shared by multiple components in an extension. For example, consider a note-taking extension that allows taking notes on any page. Initially, if only a Browser-Action is used, the entire application logic can be placed within the popup script itself. But if additional input components are added, the code inside popup script won't be accessible to these components (because a popup script is only executed when a popup is opened).

To allow for this, the shared code (reflecting the common logic) can be placed inside an event script. This allows various components to access the common application logic, without any restrictions. Obviously, the popup script (for this case) will need to use the messaging API to communicate back and forth with the event script (so as to access the common application logic). Don't get overwhelmed with this example, as you will understand it more clearly when you work out the `BrowserActionNotes` extension later in this chapter.

Role of the Manifest for This Component

To use an event script in your extension, you need to define the `background` attribute in the manifest. This attribute is an object composed of the `scripts` and `persistent` keys. The `scripts` key takes an array of strings as its value, where each string is the (relative) path to an event script. And the `persistent` key takes the Boolean `false` as its value (as displayed in Listing 2-4). Multiple event scripts are simply allowed to modularize the code (Figures 2-10 and 2-11), as shown in the following lines.

```
"background" : {
    "scripts" : ["event_script.js","another_event_script.js"],
    "persistent" : false
}
```

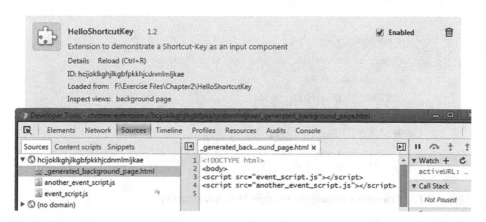

Figure 2-10. *HelloShortcutKey: Background page*

Figure 2-11. *HelloShortcutKey: Background page*

Additionally, once these script(s) are defined in the manifest—upon the successful loading of the extension (in the browser)—they are automatically referred in an auto-generated HTML page, known as the *background page*, as shown in Figures 2-12 and 2-13.

Figure 2-12. *Extensions Management page: HelloShortcutKey*

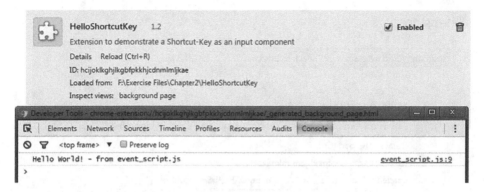

Figure 2-13. HelloShortcutKey: background page

The actual HTML file is named differently (see Figure 2-14).

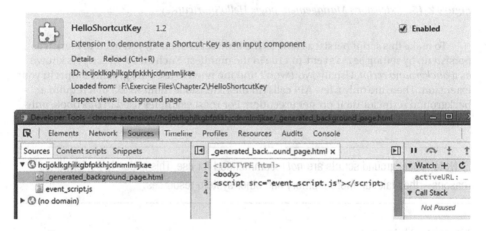

Figure 2-14. HelloShortcutKey: Background page

Background Scripts

Event scripts persist only as long as the events being listened to are getting triggered. When events are not getting triggered, event scripts are made inactive by the Chrome browser (note that this does not happen immediately), as displayed in Figure 2-15.

Extensions

Figure 2-15. *Extensions Management page: HelloShortcutKey*

To make this script persist as long as the browser is opened, you need to mark it as persistent, by setting `persistent` to `true` in the manifest. Such an event script is known as a *background script*. Usually, you won't find the need to use background scripts in your extension. There are only a few API calls (in the Extensions framework) that require a background script for their proper execution. For most examples used in this book, only event script are used unless stated otherwise.

■ **Note** Background scripts are *not* recommended for use. This is due to performance reasons—they take up more memory and other system resources.

Event Objects

In all the events discussed in the current topic, one thing is common. They all represent an event object in the Extensions framework. An *event* is an object that allows you to be notified when something interesting happens. The following is an example of using the `chrome.alarms.onAlarm` event to be notified whenever an alarm has elapsed.

```
chrome.alarms.onAlarm.addListener(function(alarm) {
    if(alarm.name == "A") {/**/}
    else if(alarm.name == "B") {/**/}
    else {/**/}
});
```

Similar to the DOM APIs, the events in the Extensions framework also require a listener function, registered using the addListener method. It should not be confused with the addEventListener method of the DOM API. Every API in the Extensions framework (browserAction, pageAction, commands, tabs, alarms, bookmarks, etc.) passes different kinds of arguments to the listener functions. For the example listed previously, the listener receives an argument of type Alarm.

Aside from the events discussed so far, the Extensions framework also provides an advanced system for taking actions depending on (matching of) certain custom rules. Although this sounds similar to the typical *events and listeners* model, it is not. This advanced feature in the Extensions framework is known as a *declarative event handler* and will be discussed in the following topic of the same name.

Revisiting the onCommand Event

Now you can finally revisit the HelloShortcutKey extension. To listen for the onCommand event, first you need to create an event script in the extension folder. An event script can be named anything you like, as long as it is a valid file name. Next, you need to list the event script in the manifest. For that, you first need to define the background manifest attribute.

Add two properties to this attribute—scripts and persistent. As mentioned earlier, the scripts attribute takes an array as its value. The event script will be listed within this array. For this extension, since you don't want the event script(s) to persist as long as the browser is opened (you only want them to stay active on an event basis), you need to define persistent as false, as displayed in Listing 2-4.

When this extension loads in the browser, the *background page* corresponding to the event script will start listening for any events. To handle the onCommand event, you need to implement its listener function (see Listing 2-5). When the defined shortcut key(s) are invoked, the *background page* will become active and execute the listener function. It will be made inactive once it goes idle (see Figure 2-11), thereby also unloading all the associated scripts (to save memory and other system resources).

Declarative Event Handlers

Before we start the discussion on declarative event handlers as an advanced mechanism to take actions based on custom rules, divert your attention to the HelloPageAction extension to display Page-Actions. This extension is provided in Chapter 2's Exercise Files folder. You can load it in the browser for testing.

Listing 2-6. Chapter2/HelloPageAction/manifest.json

```json
{
    "manifest_version" : 2,
    "name" : "HelloPageAction",
    "description" : "Extension to demonstrate a Page-Action",
    "version" : "1.2",
    "page_action" : {
        "default_title" : "HelloPageAction",
        "default_icon" : "icon.png",
```

```
        "default_popup" : "popup.html"
    },
    "background" : {
        "scripts" : ["event_script.js"],
        "persistent" : false
    },
    "permissions" : [
        "tabs"
    ]
}
```

The HelloPageAction Extension

As displayed in Listing 2-6, apart from declaring and defining the Page-Action, the manifest
for this extension also contains a definition for the background manifest attribute to use an
event script. In addition to this, the manifest also contains the permissions attribute to use
the tabs feature (you will read about the permissions attribute in Chapter 3). To make the
event script active only on an event basis, persistent is defined as false.

Listing 2-7. Chapter2/HelloPageAction/event_script.js

```javascript
//region {variables and functions}
var consoleGreeting = "Hello World! - from event_script.js";
var queryInfoForAllTabs = {
    //"active":false,"currentWindow":true
};
function logTabs(tabs) {
    console.group("Tabs");
    console.log(tabs);
    console.groupEnd("Tabs");
}
function queryTabsAndShowPageActions() {
    chrome.tabs.query(
        queryInfoForAllTabs,
        function(tabs) {
            console.log("All tabs length: %s", tabs.length);
            //Output tabs object to the console as a separate visual group
            logTabs(tabs);
            if(tabs.length > 0) {
                for(var i=0; i<tabs.length; i++) {
                    chrome.pageAction.show(tabs[i].id);
                }
            }
        }
    );
}
//end-region
```

Listings 2-7 and 2-8 contain the code for the event script used in this extension. The function queryTabsAndShowPageActions makes use of the chrome.tabs.query API to query the tabs based on the object queryInfoForAllTabs, which is passed as the first argument to the query method. This object is empty, so as to make the query API return all the tabs. This is required in your extension to show Page-Actions on all the tabs.

The second argument of the query method is a callback function, which receives tabs as its first (and only) argument. Because it is an array, you can iterate over it. Every element in this array is of Tab type. In the Chrome Extensions framework, every tab is represented using this Tab type. This type has many properties associated with it, and the important ones include id, active, and url.

For the purpose of this extension, you need the id property in order to show the Page-Action. Page-Action is displayed in a tab by calling the method chrome.pageAction. show, which takes the id of the tab as its only argument. So, inside the loop for(var i=0; i<tabs.length; i++), the show method is called to display the Page-Action.

Listing 2-8. Chapter2/HelloPageAction/event_script.js

```
//region {calls}
console.log(consoleGreeting);
//Show Page-Actions using the chrome.tabs.query method
//queryTabsAndShowPageActions();
//Show Page-Actions using the onUpdated event
chrome.tabs.onUpdated.addListener(function(tabId,changeInfo,tab) {
    chrome.pageAction.show(tabId);
});
//end-region
```

However, there is one drawback to using the queryTabsAndShowPageActions function. This function will only get called once, i.e. when the event script first loads in the browser. In order to show Page-Action every time you open (or update) a tab, this will not suffice. For that, you need to listen for an event on the tabs—the onUpdated event. The use of this event is demonstrated in Listing 2-8. For the purpose of this extension, the queryTabsAndShowPageActions function call has been commented out. Page-Actions are displayed by simply listening for the onUpdated event. This way, every time a tab gets updated (i.e., opened or updated), the listener function will get called and will display a Page-Action for the corresponding tab, with an ID of tabId (the argument received by the listener function, as shown in Listing 2-8).

The declarativeContent API

Now we can begin the discussion on declarative event handlers. Declarative event handlers provide a means to define certain rules consisting of declarative conditions and actions. Conditions are evaluated in the browser itself, rather than the JavaScript engine that powers the Extensions framework. This reduces the round-trip latencies between the browser and the (aforementioned) JavaScript engine. At the time of writing this book, there are two kinds of declarative event handlers—chrome.declarativeContent and chrome.declarativeWebRequest. For the course of this book, you won't be dealing with the latter (as it is not available to the Google Chrome users on the stable channel).

You can use the chrome.declarativeContent API to take actions depending on the content of a web page, without requiring permission to read the web page's content (which is done using content scripts that are injected into the visited web pages, to read and modify the web page's content). Only two such actions are supported at the time of writing—chrome.declarativeContent.ShowPageAction and chrome.declarativeContent.SetIcon. To use this API, the following permission is required in the manifest: declarativeContent.

Adding and Removing Rules

As a declarative API, this API lets you register rules on the onPageChanged event, i.e. using chrome.declarativeContent.onPageChanged.*. Here, * could mean addRules or removeRules. The addRules method takes an array of rule instances as its first parameter, and an optional callback function (that is called on completion) as the second parameter.

```
var rule1 = {
    id : "some_rule_A", //Optional, will be generated if not set
    priority : 100,  //Optional, defaults to 100
    conditions : [/*conditions*/],
    actions : [/*actions*/]
};
...
var ruleList = [rule1,rule2,...];
chrome.declarativeContent.onPageChanged.addRules(ruleList);
```

To remove rules, call the removeRules method. It accepts an optional array of rule identifiers (for example, [rule1.id,rule2.id]) as its first parameter, and a callback function as its second parameter. If the array is undefined, all registered rules of this extension are removed.

Listing 2-9. Chapter2/PageActionNotes/event_script.js

```
//region {variables and functions}
var consoleGreeting = "Hello World! - from event_script.js";
var ruleStackOverflowHost = {
    "conditions" : [
        new chrome.declarativeContent.PageStateMatcher({
            "pageUrl" : {
                "hostEquals" : "stackoverflow.com",
                "schemes" : ["http","https"]
            }
        })
    ],
    "actions" : [new chrome.declarativeContent.ShowPageAction()]
};
//end-region
```

■ **Note** Rules are persistent across browsing sessions. Therefore, you should add rules during extension installation time, using the `runtime.onInstalled` event. Note that this event is also triggered when an extension is updated. Therefore, you should first clear previously installed rules and then register new rules. For more details on rules, visit the following URL `https://developer.chrome.com/extensions/events`.

Listing 2-10. Chapter2/PageActionNotes/event_script.js

```
//region {calls}
console.log(consoleGreeting);
chrome.runtime.onInstalled.addListener(function() {
    //Replace all rules
    chrome.declarativeContent.onPageChanged.removeRules(undefined,function()
{
        //With a new rule
        chrome.declarativeContent.onPageChanged.addRules(
            [ruleStackOverflowHost]
        );
    });
});
//end-region
```

Using ShowPageAction

In the previous topic, "HelloPageAction Extension," it was demonstrated how Page-Action can be displayed using the `chrome.tabs.query` method and using the `chrome.tabs.onUpdated` event. Now, you will examine another way to do so using a declarative event handlers' actions.

■ **Note** For advanced coverage of this topic, visit the URL `https://developer.chrome.com/extensions/declarativeContent`.

As displayed in Listing 2-9, the rule `ruleStackOverflowHost` is created using a condition and a corresponding action. The condition is represented using a `PageStateMatcher` object. `PageStateMatcher` matches web pages if and only if all listed criteria are met. In Listing 2-9, those criteria include `pageUrl.hostEquals` and `pageUrl.schemes` (to match all the web pages on `stackoverflow.com`). In addition to using the `pageUrl` criteria, `css` criteria can also be used. For example, consider the following rule to show a Page-Action for web pages on `https://www.google.com/`, when a password field is present on it:

```
var rule1 = {
    "conditions" : [
        new chrome.declarativeContent.PageStateMatcher({
```

```
            "pageUrl" : {
                "hostEquals" : "www.google.com",
                "schemes" : ["https"]
            },
            "css" : ["input[type='password']"]
        })
    ],
    "actions" : [new chrome.declarativeContent.ShowPageAction()]
};
```

As discussed already, only two actions are supported by the declarativeContent
API. An action is listed as an element of the actions array (actions is an attribute of the
rule instance, as displayed in Listing 2-9). Finally, to register the rules, the following calls
are made. As rules are persistent across browsing sessions, they are only added once,
which is when the extension installs. Additionally, to clear all the previously defined rules,
removeRules is called with undefined as the first argument.

```
chrome.runtime.onInstalled.addListener(function() {
    //Replace all rules
    chrome.declarativeContent.onPageChanged.removeRules(undefined,function() {
        //With a new rule
        chrome.declarativeContent.onPageChanged.addRules(
            [ruleStackOverflowHost]
        );
    });
});
```

Content Scripts

In the previous topic on the declarativeContent API, you understood how without
reading the web page contents you can take certain actions simply by declaring some
condition(s). This may not be always sufficient, as the declarativeContent API (via the
PageStateMatcher object) only allows certain limited criteria for matching. Moreover, the
actions are also very limited. This is where content scripts are useful.

Content scripts are a type of scripting component that is injected into the visited web
page(s). They have a very limited access to the Chrome Extensions API (as they do not
represent the extension runtime). But, they can read and modify the contents (i.e., HTML
elements) of visited web pages using the DOM API. Since they have access to the DOM
API, they can also add content (i.e., HTML elements) to the web pages they are injected
into. Such a UI created using content scripts is known as Content UI. Before you learn
more about content scripts, keep in mind that content scripts cannot:

- Use chrome.* APIs with the exception of the following:

  - extension (getURL, inIncognitoContext, lastError,
    onRequest, sendRequest)

- i18n
- runtime (connect, getManifest, getURL, id, onConnect, onMessage, sendMessage)
- storage
- Use variables or functions defined in other scripting components.
- Use variables or functions defined by web pages (they are injected into) or by other content scripts.

■ **Note**   Content scripts can indirectly use the complete chrome.* APIs and indirectly also access the variables and functions defined in other scripting components. They can do all this by using the messaging API (discussed in Chapter 3).

Role of the Manifest for This Component

Now let's see how to configure the manifest for using the content script component. If the content scripts' code always needs to be injected automatically, you need to declare and define the content_scripts attribute in the manifest, as displayed in the following code.

```
"content_scripts" : [
    {
        "matches" : ["http://www.google.com/*"],
        "css" : ["mystyles_A.css"],
        "js" : ["jquery.js","myscript_A.js"]
    }
]
```

This attribute is an array, where each element (a content script) takes the following properties in its definition—matches, css, and js. Quite obviously, css and js are arrays of CSS and JavaScript files (respectively) that need be injected in the web pages that match against the URLs specified in the matches array.

In addition to this, JavaScript (or CSS) code can also be injected programmatically using the tabs API (which requires the tabs permission in the manifest to grant access to all the tabs for interacting with them; however, if only the currently active tab needs be accessed, the activeTab permission will suffice).

For programmatic-injection, either tabs or activeTab permission can be used in the manifest. The activeTab permission gives an extension temporary access to the currently active tab when the user invokes the extension, for example, by clicking its Browser-Action. Access to the tab lasts until the tab is navigated or closed.

The `activeTab` permission can be used when your code in the extension runtime has access to the currently active tab via the listener function(s) (say listener function for events `chrome.browserAction.onClicked` or `chrome.pageAction.onClicked`) and wants to interact with this tab by injecting JavaScript or CSS code. To interact with the remaining tabs, use the `tabs` permission. The following methods (in the `tabs` API) are used to inject CSS and JavaScript code, respectively.

```
chrome.tabs.insertCSS(integer tabId, object details, function callback)
chrome.tabs.executeScript(integer tabId, object details, function callback)
```

■ **Note**   Programmatic-injection is useful when your JavaScript or CSS code shouldn't be injected into every single web page that matches the `matches` pattern. Instead, it needs to be injected only for certain cases. For example, upon clicking of a Browser-Action or Page-Action button.

The `tabId` parameter is the ID of the tab in which to inject the CSS or JavaScript code; it defaults to the (currently) active tab of the current window. The `details` parameter is an object that contains the details of the (CSS/JavaScript) code or file to inject. In this object, the `code` or the `file` property must be set, but both may *not* be set at the same time. The `HelloContentScript` extension in Chapter 2's `Exercise Files` folder demonstrates the use of content scripts in an extension.

Listing 2-11. Chapter2/HelloContentScript/manifest.json

```json
{
    "manifest_version" : 2,
    "name" : "HelloContentScript",
    "description" : "Extension to demonstrate a content-script",
    "version" : "1.2",
    "content_scripts" : [
        {
            "matches" : ["*://stackoverflow.com/*"],
            "js" : ["content_script.js"]
        }
    ],
    "background" : {
        "scripts" : ["event_script.js"],
        "persistent" : false
    },
    "permissions" : ["activeTab"],
    "browser_action" : {
        "default_icon" : "icon.png"
    }
}
```

HelloContentScript Extension

This extension injects content scripts both the ways—using the `content_scripts` attribute in the manifest as well as using programmatic-injection (from an event script). First, let's examine the former. Note the `matches` pattern in Listing 2-11. The asterisk (*) in the beginning of the pattern represents any scheme—`http`, `https`, etc. Similarly, the asterisk in the end of the pattern represents all paths on the `stackoverflow.com` host. As displayed in Figure 2-16, the content script (`content_script.js`) gets injected upon visiting the aforementioned host. You can try out this extension and visit other paths on the `stackoverflow.com` host.

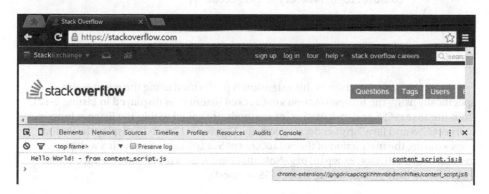

Figure 2-16. *Injected content script component*

Listing 2-12. Chapter2/HelloContentScript/event_script.js

```
//region {variables and functions}
var consoleGreeting = "Hello World! - from event_script.js";
var cssCode = "a {text-decoration:underline !important;}";
cssCode += "div {background-color:#999 !important;}";
var javascriptCode = "var imgElement = document.createElement('img');";
javascriptCode += "imgElement.src = 'http://placehold.it/350x150';";
javascriptCode += "document.body.appendChild(imgElement);";
//end-region

//region {calls}
console.log(consoleGreeting);
chrome.browserAction.onClicked.addListener(function(tab) {
    chrome.tabs.insertCSS(
        {
            //CSS file or code to inject
            //file : "mystyles.css",
            code : cssCode
        },
        function() {
            console.log("CSS inserted!");
```

65

```
        }
    );
    chrome.tabs.executeScript(
        {
            //JavaScript file or code to inject
            //file : "content_script.js",
            code : javascriptCode

        },
        function() {
            console.log("JavaScript executed!");
        }
    );
});
//end-region
```

Programmatic-injection in this extension is performed using the event script, specifically using the Browser-Action's onClicked listener (as displayed in Listing 2-12). Both the insertCSS and executeScript methods are called within the listener function to inject CSS and JavaScript code, respectively. Figures 2-17 to 2-19 display the various stages during the interaction of the HelloContentScript extension with a web page, located at the URL www.example.org. Note that Figure 2-18 represents the incomplete extension (it only contained the insertCSS method).

Example Domain

This domain is established to be used for illustrative examples in documents. You may use this domain in examples without prior coordination or asking for permission.

More information...

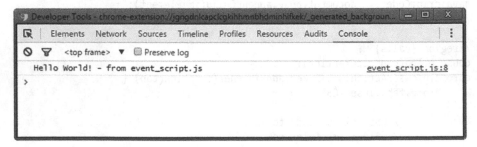

Figure 2-17. *HelloContentScript: Background page*

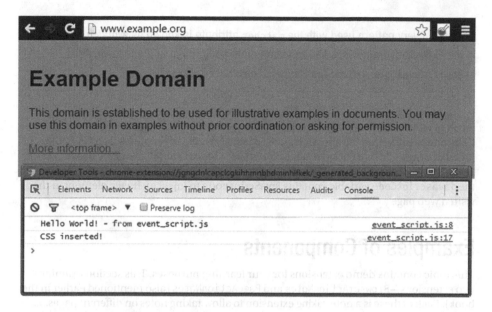

Figure 2-18. *HelloContentScript: Background page*

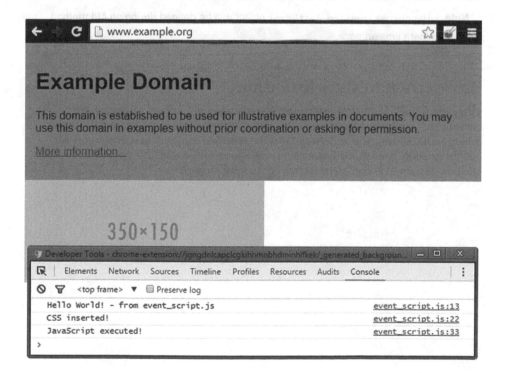

Figure 2-19. *HelloContentScript: Background page*

■ **Note** Every pattern used with the `matches` attribute is known as a *match pattern* in the Extensions framework. You can learn more about them at the following URL `https://developer.chrome.com/extensions/match_patterns`.

Upon clicking the Browser-Action button, the listener function gets called, as a result of which CSS and JavaScript codes get injected. The `cssCode` variable contains CSS code to underline the anchor tags, i.e. a tag, and code to set the background color for all `div` tags—"div {background-color:#999 !important;}". Note the use of `!important` to override any (similar) existing styles on the visited web page. Similarly, the `javascriptCode` variable contains JavaScript code to inject an image element in the visited web page.

Examples of Components

This topic contains demo extensions for your learning purposes. This section examines two extensions—`BrowserActionNotes` and `PageActionNotes` (also mentioned earlier in the book). Each of these is a note-taking extension to allow taking notes on different pages.

■ **Note** The `chrome.runtime.lastError` object will be defined during an API method callback if there was an error.

BrowserActionNotes Extension

This extension allows taking notes on all visited web pages. It uses a Browser-Action input component (as displayed in Figure 2-20) and a popup component (Figure 2-21) with a popup script. By now you understand that the manifest component is mandatory for every extension. Note that this extension only allows saving one note for a URL. The note can be overwritten or completely removed from the storage.

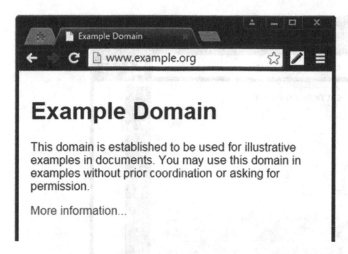

Figure 2-20. BrowserActionNotes: Browser-Action component

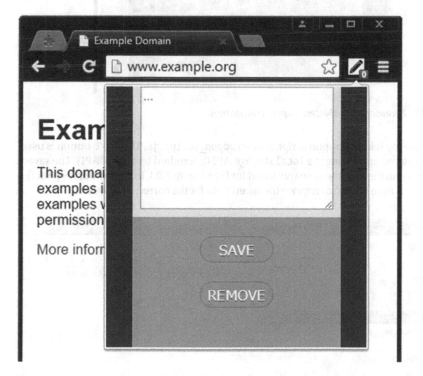

Figure 2-21. BrowserActionNotes: popup component

The popup contains a `textarea` and two buttons—SAVE and REMOVE. The `textarea` is used to contain the note to be saved (as displayed in Figure 2-22). Listing 2-13 provides the relevant code for the popup. Note the use of the `textarea` and `button` tags.

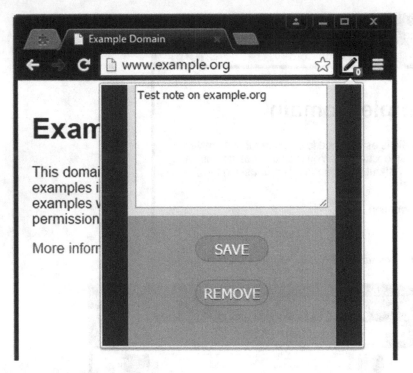

Figure 2-22. BrowserActionNotes: popup component

Also note the referred popup script, named popup_script.js. The SAVE button is used to save the entered note, using the localStorage API (a standard JavaScript API). The saved note is mapped to the URL the note was saved for (see Figure 2-23, in the Resources panel). The REMOVE button is used to remove the saved note for the corresponding URL.

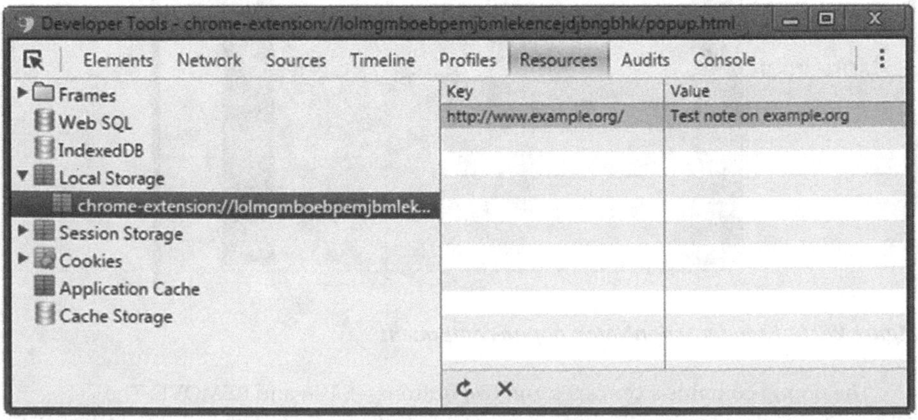

Figure 2-23. BrowserActionNotes: Resources panel

Listing 2-13. Chapter2/BrowserActionNotes/popup.html

```html
<script src="popup_script.js"></script>

<style>
...
</style>
</head>
<body>
    <div id="container">
        <div id="top"><textarea id="note" placeholder="..."></textarea></div>
        <div id="bottom">
            <br>
            <button id="save_button">SAVE</button>
            <br>
            <button id="remove_button">REMOVE</button>
        </div>
    </div>
</body>
</html>
```

The popup script, upon loading, gets references to the textarea and button elements. This is done using the getElementById method (a Standard JavaScript API). The most important functions defined in the popup script (see Listing 2-14) are hardSave and removeNote. Both these functions use the tab's API to access the currently active tab. Note that this extension uses the tabs permission in the manifest.

Upon clicking of the saveButton in the popup, the hardSave function gets called. Similarly, clicking the removeButton calls the removeNote function. A note is saved by calling the localStorage.setItem method—"localStorage.setItem(activeURL,noteText)". It is removed by calling the localStorage.removeItem method.

Listing 2-14. Chapter2/BrowserActionNotes/popup_script.js

```javascript
//region {variables and functions}
var consoleGreeting = "Hello World! - from popup_script.js";
//Active-URL can also be cached
//var activeURL = "";
var noteElementID = "note";
var saveButtonID = "save_button";
var removeButtonID = "remove_button";
var noteElement = null;
var saveButton = null;
var removeButton = null;
var queryInfo = {"active":true};
function logSuccess(task) {
    console.log("%s Successful!",task);
    chrome.browserAction.setBadgeText({"text":localStorage.length.toString()});
}
```

71

```
//function logFailure(task) {console.log("%s Failed!",task);}
function loadNoteForActiveURL(noteElement) {
    chrome.tabs.query(queryInfo,function(tabs) {
        var activeURL = tabs[0].url;
        noteElement.value = localStorage.getItem(activeURL);
        logSuccess("Get-Storage");
    });
}
function softSave(noteText) {} //appends the text
function hardSave(noteText) { //overwrites the text
    chrome.tabs.query(queryInfo,function(tabs) {
        var activeURL = tabs[0].url;
        localStorage.setItem(activeURL,noteText);
        logSuccess("Set-Storage");
    });
}
function removeNote() {
        chrome.tabs.query(queryInfo,function(tabs) {
        var activeURL = tabs[0].url;
        localStorage.removeItem(activeURL);
        logSuccess("Remove-Storage");
    });
}
//end-region
```

As soon as the popup opens, the loadNoteForActiveURL function (Listing 2-15) gets called to access the note corresponding to the currently active URL and to load this note in the textarea element. Note the use of the logSuccess function. Aside from use as a logging function, it is also used to set the badge text for the Browser-Action (see Figures 2-24 and 2-25). This text is updated with the localStorage.length value, at various times when you interact with the extension.

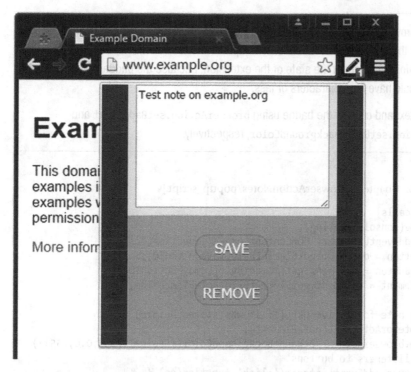

Figure 2-24. BrowserActionNotes: Setting the badge text

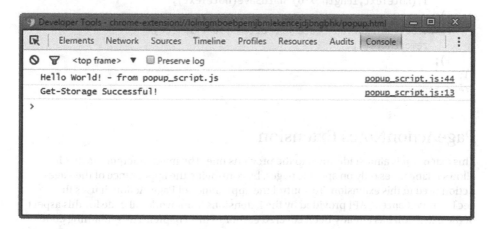

Figure 2-25. BrowserActionNotes: Console panel for popup

■ **Note**   Browser-Actions can optionally display a badge, which is a bit of text that is layered over the icon. Badges make it easy to update the Browser-Action to display a small amount of information about the state of the extension. Because the badge has limited space, it should have four characters or less.

You set the text and color of the badge using `browserAction.setBadgeText` and `browserAction.setBadgeBackgroundColor`, respectively.

Listing 2-15. Chapter2/BrowserActionNotes/popup_script.js

```javascript
//region {calls}
console.log(consoleGreeting);
document.addEventListener('DOMContentLoaded',function(dcle) {
    saveButton = document.getElementById(saveButtonID);
    removeButton = document.getElementById(removeButtonID);
    noteElement = document.getElementById(noteElementID);

    //Load note for active URL (if it was stored before)
    loadNoteForActiveURL(noteElement);
    chrome.browserAction.setBadgeBackgroundColor({"color":[255,0,0,255]})
    //Add listeners to buttons
    saveButton.addEventListener('click',function(ce) {
        var noteText = noteElement.value;
        if(noteText.length > 0) hardSave(noteText);
    });
    removeButton.addEventListener('click',function(ce) {
        removeNote();
    });
});
//end-region
```

PageActionNotes Extension

This extension is almost identical to the previous one. The main difference is that it allows taking notes only on specific pages, by controlling the appearance of the Page-Action used in this extension. To control the appearance of Page-Action, it uses the `declarativeContent` API provided by the Extensions framework. All code for this aspect of the extension has already been covered earlier in this chapter. The remaining code (for the popup and popup script components) is identical to the previous extension. Hence, we are only left with discussing the flow of this extension.

As displayed in Figure 2-26, this extension has an event script component. The event script (Listings 2-9 and 2-10) contains the code to register the rules to allow the appearance of Page-Action only on web pages belonging to the `stackoverflow.com` host.

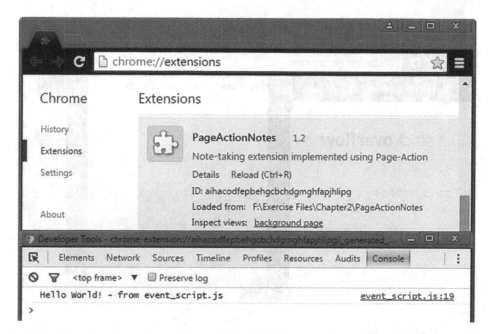

Figure 2-26. *PageActionNotes: background page*

The Page-Action, along with the popup, is displayed in Figures 2-27 to 2-29.

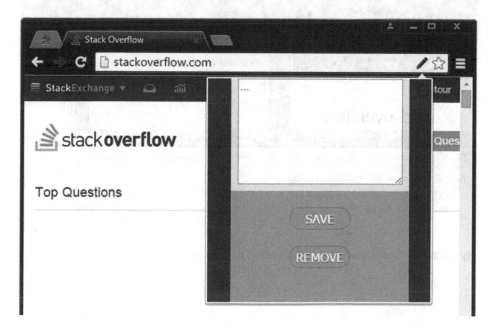

Figure 2-27. *PageActionNotes: Popup component*

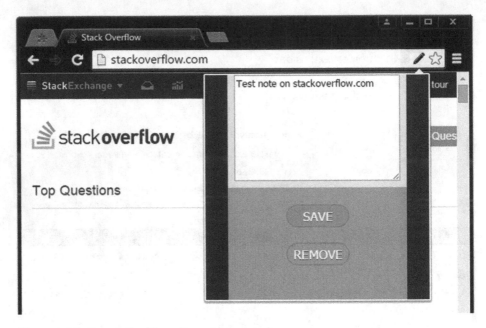

Figure 2-28. *PageActionNotes: Popup component*

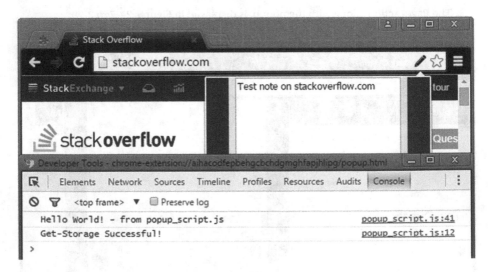

Figure 2-29. *PageActionNotes: Console panel for popup*

This way, when any web page belonging to the `stackoverflow.com` host is visited, Page-Action button will be displayed. Upon clicking the Page-Action, the popup will open. As discussed, this popup (along with its popup script) is identical to the popup used in the previous extension. This popup will allow you to interact with the `textarea`, to enter the note to be saved. And finally, clicking the SAVE button will save the note. Once again, you can visit the Resources panel to confirm the storage of the note. When you revisit the URL for which a note was already saved, opening the popup will automatically load the note in the `textarea` (as displayed in Figure 2-29).

Summary

In this chapter you learned that there are certain components used to create an extension. These include the manifest component (which is a must-have for every extension!), the input component(s), the scripting component(s), and an optional popup component. You also learned about the lifecycle of an extension, where you understood the use of event scripts to listen for various events fired from input components, as well as events that are fired from feature API (i.e., APIs such as `tabs`, `alarms`, `storage`, `bookmarks`, `history`, etc.).

You also learned why only event scripts are used to represent the extension runtime, by listing their many advantages over popup scripts (that are only executed when a popup is opened). You learned why input components are necessary in an extension, as they provide an entry point (for the users) to interact with. Remember, though, that fully functional extensions can be created without any input components!

Finally, you learned about the `declarativeContent` API to register custom rules in an extension and also the `content-script` component, to inject JavaScript and CSS files into visited web pages (in a declarative, as well as in a programmatic, manner).

In the next chapter, you will read about various APIs provided by the Chrome Extensions framework. You will also learn about messaging APIs to communicate between different scripting components, as well as between web page scripts and scripting components.

CHAPTER 3

API Availability and Messaging

This chapter describes the various ways in which scripting components can interact with each other using the messaging APIs provided by the Google Chrome Extensions framework. In addition to this, you will also learn how ordinary web pages can interact with an extension. Plus, you will also examine the usage of many useful APIs provided by the Extensions framework. But before all of this, first you will learn about the remaining input components.

Like the previous chapters, this chapter assumes you have some experience of writing simple web pages using technologies such as HTML, CSS, and JavaScript. You should know the event-driven nature of web pages, for example—showing some UI after clicking a button (using event listeners), etc. In addition to this, you should also know about the architecture of extensions, which is comprised of components, such as manifest file, inputs, scripts, and popups. That said, let's begin!

Input Components: Part Two

The previous chapter left out some input components to discuss. This section takes them on before you start examining various APIs in the Extensions framework and understanding the messaging APIs. The input components that are discussed here include the omnibox input and the context menu item. In addition to these components, the application of the Content UI component is also discussed.

Omnibox Inputs

The omnibox input is a very special input component that allows you to register a keyword with Google Chrome's address bar, which is also known as the *omnibox*. Using this input component is extremely easy, as it only requires an event script component and a small addition to the manifest, as follows:

```
"omnibox" : {
    "keyword" : "OI"
}
```

© Prateek Mehta 2016

P. Mehta, *Creating Google Chrome Extensions*, DOI 10.1007/978-1-4842-1775-7_3

As shown, to use the omnibox input component, the omnibox manifest attribute is required. This attribute has a keyword property. When the corresponding keyword value (in this case, OI), which is case-insensitive, is entered into the address bar (upon certain confirmation), the user can begin interacting solely with the extension. This is displayed in Figures 3-2 and 3-3.

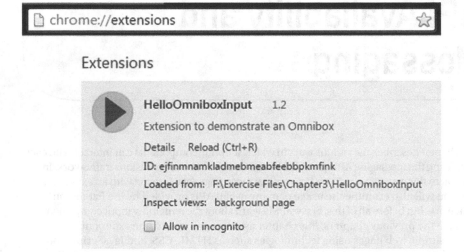

Figure 3-1. *Extensions Management Page: HelloOmniboxInput*

Additionally, to use an icon in the address bar, when the user is interacting, you can define the icons attribute in the manifest (see Listing 3-1). Note that Chrome automatically creates a grayscale version of the 16px icon listed in the manifest. Also see Figures 3-1 and 3-3 to note the difference between colored and grayscaled versions of the icon.

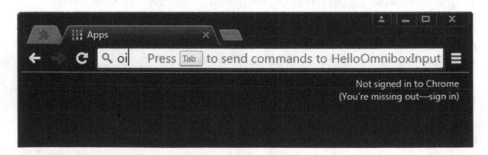

Figure 3-2. *HelloOmniboxInput: Entering the keyword*

Listing 3-1. Chapter3/HelloOmniboxInput/manifest.json

```
{
    "manifest_version" : 2,
    "version" : "1.2",
    "name" : "HelloOmniboxInput",
    "description" : "Extension to demonstrate an Omnibox",
    "background" : {
        "scripts" : ["event_script.js"],
        "persistent" : false
    },
    "omnibox" : {
        "keyword" : "OI"
    },
    "icons" : {
        "16" : "icon-16.png",
        "128" : "icon-128.png"
    }
}
```

Role of an Event Script for this Component

Now for the event script part needed to use this input component. Similar to the use of event script for other input components, for the omnibox input component also, an event script is used to listen for the associated events. These events include onInputStarted, onInputChanged, onInputEntered, and onInputCancelled. Note that these events belong to the chrome.omnibox API. This API does not require any permission in the manifest. The use of these events is demonstrated in Listing 3-2.

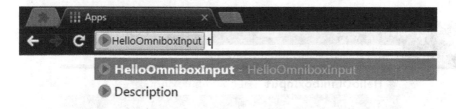

Figure 3-3. *HelloOmniboxInput: Interacting with the omnibox*

Listing 3-2. Chapter3/HelloOmniboxInput/event_script.js

```
//region {variables and functions}
var ON_INPUT_ENTERED_DISPOSITION = {
    "CURRENT_TAB" : "currentTab",
    "NEW_FOREGROUND_TAB" : "newForegroundTab",
    "NEW_BACKGROUND_TAB" : "newBackgroundTab"
};
```

```
var suggestResultOne = {
    "content" : "Some content",
    "description" : "Description"
};
var suggestResults = [suggestResultOne];
var searchService = "https://www.google.com/";
searchService += "search?q=chrome+extensions+developers+";
function CreateWindow(url) {
    var windowCreateData = {"url" : ""};
    windowCreateData.url = url;
    chrome.windows.create(windowCreateData);
}
//end-region

//region {calls}
chrome.omnibox.onInputStarted.addListener(function() {
    console.log("<InputStarted>");
});
chrome.omnibox.onInputChanged.addListener(function(text,suggest) {
    console.log("<InputChanged> Text: " + text);
    //suggest(suggestResults);
    suggest(getSuggestResults(text));
});
chrome.omnibox.onInputEntered.addListener(function(text,disposition) {
    console.log("<InputEntered> Text: " + text);
    CreateWindow(searchService + text);
    //default disposition is ON_INPUT_ENTERED_DISPOSITION.CURRENT_TAB
});
//end-region
```

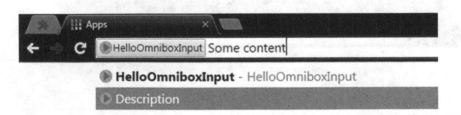

Figure 3-4. *HelloOmniboxInput: Suggested results*

The most important events that need to be listened to are chrome.omnibox.
onInputChanged, and chrome.omnibox.onInputEntered. Firing of the former (event)
means that the user has changed what is typed into the omnibox, and the latter
(i.e., onInputEntered event) means that the user has accepted what is typed, or
suggested, into the omnibox. The logs associated with different events can be seen in
Figure 3-6.

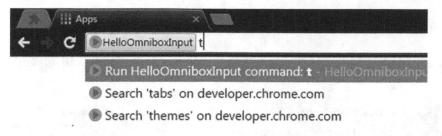

Figure 3-5. *HelloOmniboxInput: Interacting with the omnibox*

When onInputChanged event gets fired, you need to suggest results for the user to accept. Results can be suggested by passing an array to the suggest callback (see Listing 3-2). Note that each element in this array should be of type SuggestResult, which is an object with the content and description properties. For example, to suggest a result suggestResultOne, which is defined as

```
var suggestResultOne = {"content":"Some content","description":
"Description"};
```

You need to pass the array [suggestResultOne] to the suggest callback. Figures 3-4 and 3-5 show suggestion of results, where the suggested results are Description and Search 'tabs' on ..., Search 'themes' on ... for Figures 3-4 and 3-5, respectively. Note that what actually gets accepted is the content corresponding to these descriptions. And by getting "accepted," I mean, passing of the content to the listener function for the onInputEntered event.

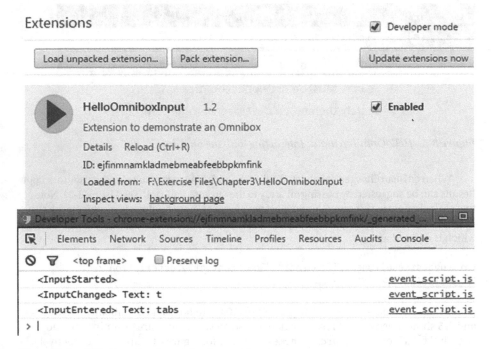

Figure 3-6. *HelloOmniboxInput: background page*

The content is passed to this listener function as the text parameter, shown in Listing 3-2. The second parameter, called disposition, is the recommended context to display results. This is usually not required, as it has a default value of current tab. The text, in Listing 3-2, is used to display related search web pages in a new window. Note the use of the chrome.windows.create method to create a new window (see Figure 3-8).

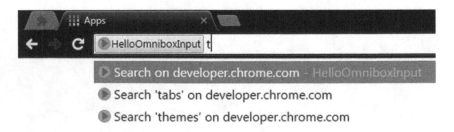

Figure 3-7. *HelloOmniboxInput: Setting the default suggestion*

Note the default suggestion Run HelloOmniboxInput command... seen in Figure 3-5, for the HelloOmniboxInput extension. This can be easily overridden to Search on developer.chrome.com (displayed in Figure 3-7) by executing the following lines of code in the event script component:

```
chrome.omnibox.setDefaultSuggestion(
    {"description":"Search on developer.chrome.com"}
);
```

Context Menu Items

In the Chrome Extensions framework, one of the most advanced and feature-leveraging input component provided is the context menu item. This component allows an extension to create item(s) in the context menu, as displayed in Figure 3-10. The created item can nest other such items within itself. This becomes extremely useful when an extension offers multiple related functionalities (each displayed as a separate context menu item) that can be grouped under a single item. This input component requires the contextMenus permission.

Listing 3-3. Chapter3/HelloContextMenuItem/manifest.json

```
{
    "manifest_version" : 2,
    "name" : "HelloContextMenuItem",
    "description" : "Extension to demonstrate a Context-Menu-Item",
    "version" : "1.2",
    "permissions" : ["contextMenus"],
    "icons" : {
        "16" : "icon-16.png",
        "128" : "icon-128.png"
    },
    "background" : {
        "scripts" : ["event_script.js"],
        "persistent" : true
    }
}
```

Similar to the input component discussed in the previous topic, using the context menu item component is also very straightforward. First, you need to use the contextMenus permission in the manifest. Then, you need to use an event script component in order to create item(s) in the context menu. This event script component needs to be defined with persistent set to true in the manifest, in order to make it persist as long as the browser is opened. This is required because the item(s) in the context menu are defined from within the event script component, so it should last long enough. The corresponding code for the event script component and the contextMenus permission is provided in Listing 3-3.

■ **Note**   Recall, that an event script with `persistent` defined as `true` is a *background script,* as discussed in Chapter 2.

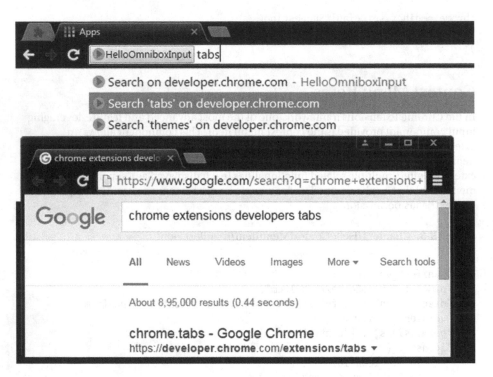

Figure 3-8.   *HelloOmniboxInput: Setting the default suggestion*

Creating an Item

There are different forms of context menu items, including `normal`, `separator`, `checkbox`, etc. Here, you will create a "normal" item. Note that if your extension requires the use of multiple items in the context menu, you can also use a "separator" item to (visually) group your items.

■ **Note**   A context menu item can take different forms. It can be a "normal" item (the typical item you always notice in context menus), a "separator" item, a "checkbox" item, or a "radio" item. For the course of this book, we will be dealing only with the first-two items. This will help you focus more on the various contexts available to context menus in the Chrome browser.

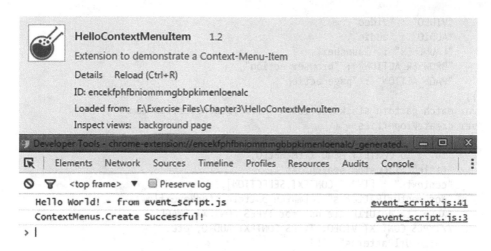

Figure 3-9. *HelloContextMenuItem: background page*

Every context menu item is identified using a unique ID. In Listing 3-4, this is defined using the ID_CONTEXT_MENU_ITEM_HELLO variable. Next are the different types of contexts an item can appear in. The different types of contexts are defined using the TYPES_CONTEXT variable in Listing 3-4. Note that the browser_action and page_action contexts are associated with the buttons for these actions, as well as their popup components. The remaining contexts have their usual meanings. We won't be dealing with the launcher context.

Listing 3-4. Chapter3/HelloContextMenuItem/event_script.js

```
//region {variables and functions}
var consoleGreeting = "Hello World! - from event_script.js";
function logSuccess(task) {console.log("%s Successful!",task);}
function logFailure(task) {console.log("%s Failed!",task);}
var ID_CONTEXT_MENU_ITEM_HELLO = "ID_CONTEXT_MENU_ITEM_HELLO";
var TYPES_CONTEXT_MENU_ITEM = { //Object used as an enum
    "NORMAL" : "normal",
    "CHECKBOX" : "checkbox",
    "RADIO" : "radio",
    "SEPARATOR" : "separator"
};
var TYPES_CONTEXT = {
    "ALL" : "all",
    "PAGE" : "page",
    "FRAME" : "frame",
    "SELECTION" : "selection",
    "LINK" : "link",
    "EDITABLE" : "editable",
    "IMAGE" : "image",
```

```
    "VIDEO" : "video",
    "AUDIO" : "audio",
    "LAUNCHER" : "launcher",
    "BROWSER_ACTION" : "browser_action",
    "PAGE_ACTION" : "page_action"
};
var match_pattern_stackoverflow = "*://*.stackoverflow.com/*";
var createProperties = {
    "type" : TYPES_CONTEXT_MENU_ITEM.NORMAL,
    "id" : ID_CONTEXT_MENU_ITEM_HELLO,
    "title" : "Custom search '%s'",
    "contexts" : [TYPES_CONTEXT.SELECTION],
    "documentUrlPatterns" : [match_pattern_stackoverflow],
    //Use "targetUrlPatterns" for TYPES_CONTEXT.IMAGE,
    //TYPES_CONTEXT.VIDEO, TYPES_CONTEXT.AUDIO, etc.
    "targetUrlPatterns" : []
};
//end-region
```

The event script code seen in Listings 3-4 and 3-5 is from the HelloContextMenuItem extension. In this extension, a context menu item is created only when a selection is made in the visited web page (see Figure 3-10). Additionally, to allow this only on the stackoverflow.com host, the documentUrlPatterns property is also defined in the createProperties object, as shown in Listing 3-4.

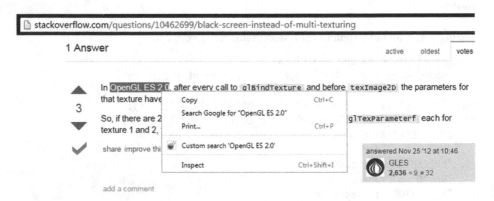

Figure 3-10. *HelloContextMenuItem: Context menu item component*

Listing 3-5. Chapter3/HelloContextMenuItem/event_script.js

```
//region {calls}
console.log(consoleGreeting);
chrome.contextMenus.create(createProperties,function() {
    if(!chrome.runtime.lastError) {
        logSuccess("ContextMenus.Create");
        chrome.contextMenus.onClicked.addListener(
            function(info,tab) {
                console.log(
                    "id: %s, selection: %s, url: %s",
                    info.menuItemId,info.selectionText,
                    tab.url
                );
            }
        );
    } else {
        logFailure("ContextMenus.Create");
    }
});
//end-region
```

There are two stages to using this component—the first is creating the context menu item (Figure 3-9 shows the corresponding log) and the second is listening for the onClicked event on this item. Creating the context menu item is done using the chrome. contextMenus.create method. This method takes an object as its first parameter, to create a context menu item with the defined properties. If the creation is not successful, the chrome.runtime.lastError object gets defined to the last error that was caused. Conversely, if the creation is successful, you can define the listener function for the onClicked event, as shown in Listing 3-5.

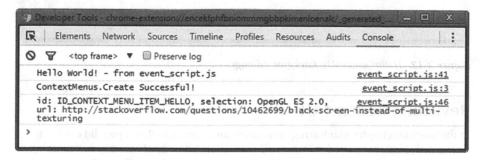

Figure 3-11. *HelloContextMenuItem: Background page*

89

Note that this listener receives an info object, as well as the tab object (which is of Tab type). The info object contains important information when a context menu item is clicked. This information can be used to take actions depending on the item that was clicked. For example, in Listing 3-5, the info.menuItemId property is simply logged to the console (Figure 3-11 shows the corresponding log).

Other important properties include parentMenuItemId, mediaType, linkUrl, selectionText, etc. The complete list of properties is available at the URL https:// developer.chrome.com/extensions/contextMenus.

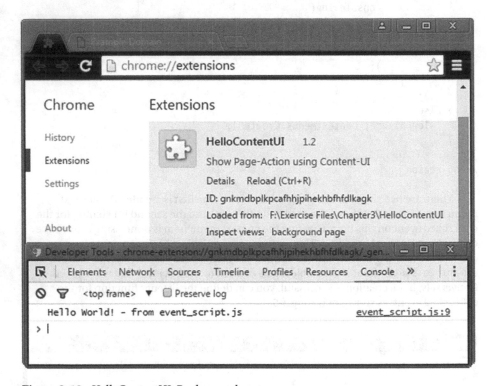

Figure 3-12. *HelloContentUI: Background page*

Revisiting Content-UI

In the previous chapter, you learned how to create a Content-UI. But you did not learn how exactly it might be used or interacted with, apart from simply staying as a static content on the web page (see Figure 2-19) it is injected into. You will examine its use with the help of the HelloContentUI extension, which is provided in Chapter 3's Exercise Files folder. In this extension, Content-UI is used to display the Page-Action component.

■ **Note** The accompanying source code for this book is available (for free) in the
Downloads section at http://www.apress.com/9781484217740.

The HelloContentUI Extension

This extension contains a content script component that is injected into the visited web
pages belonging to the example.org host, as inferred from the matches attribute in its
manifest, which is in Listing 3-6. In addition to this, it also contains a Page-Action and an
event script component (see Figure 3-12). Note the use of activeTab permission to only
interact with the currently active tab (in this case, via the content script component).

Listing 3-6. Chapter3/HelloContentUI/manifest.json

```
{
    "manifest_version" : 2,
    "name" : "HelloContentUI",
    "description" : "Show Page-Action using Content-UI",
    "version" : "1.2",
    "page_action" : {
        "default_title" : "HelloContentUI",
        "default_icon" : "icon.png",
        "default_popup" : "popup.html"
    },
    "background" : {
        "scripts" : ["event_script.js"],
        "persistent" : false
    },
    "permissions" : [
        "activeTab"
    ],
    "content_scripts" : [
        {
            "matches" : ["*://www.example.org/*"],
            "js" : ["content_script.js"]
        }
    ]
}
```

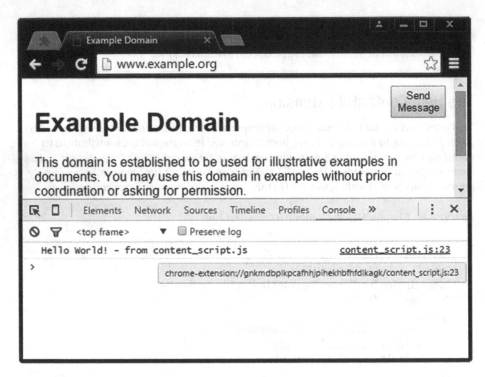

Figure 3-13. *HelloContentUI: Injected content script component*

Listing 3-7. Chapter3/HelloContentUI/content_script.js

```
//region {variables and functions}
var consoleGreeting = "Hello World! - from content_script.js";
var requestMessage = {"data":"Test message X"};
var responseCallback = function(responseMessage) {
    console.log("responseMessage: " + responseMessage.data);
};
function createButton() {
    var button = document.createElement("button");
    button.style.width = "70px";
    button.style.height = "40px";
    button.style.position = "fixed";
    button.style.top = "10px";
    button.style.right = "10px";
    button.innerText = "Send Message";
    document.body.appendChild(button);
    return button;
}
//end-region
```

```
//region {calls}
console.log(consoleGreeting);
var button = createButton();
button.addEventListener("click",function() {
    console.log("Button clicked!");
    chrome.runtime.sendMessage(/*extensionId,*/
        requestMessage,
        responseCallback
    );
});
//end-region
```

As displayed in Figure 3-13, the content script component (content_script.js) is used to create a button element ("Send Message") into the web page it is injected into. The addEventListener method (see Listing 3-7) is used to provide a callback to handle the click event on this button (recall from Chapter 2 that a content script component has access to all the standard JavaScript APIs). Page-Action will get displayed upon clicking this button. You might wonder how this works. Well, this is where the messaging APIs become useful. As described, the messaging APIs, provided in the Extensions framework, allow different scripting components to interact with each other. This is displayed in Listings 3-7 and 3-8.

The content script component in this extension uses the runtime.sendMessage method of the messaging API to send a message to the extension runtime. Recall that an event script is used to represent the extension runtime (refer back to the topic "Scripts Representing Runtime" to remind yourself of the extension runtime).

Listing 3-8. Chapter3/HelloContentUI/event_script.js

```
//region {variables and functions}
var consoleGreeting = "Hello World! - from event_script.js";
var responseMessage = {"data":"Test message Y"};
//end-region

//region {calls}
console.log(consoleGreeting);
//Show Page-Action using the onMessage event
chrome.runtime.onMessage.addListener(
    function(requestMessage,sender,sendResponse) {
        chrome.pageAction.show(sender.tab.id);
        console.log("requestMessage: " + requestMessage.data);
        sendResponse(responseMessage);
    }
);
//end-region
```

As displayed in Listing 3-8, the event script component (event_script.js) can listen for the messages using the listener function for the runtime.onMessage event. In this case, the listener function contains code to display the Page-Action (see Figure 3-14) for the corresponding tab, which is obtained from the sender object's tab ID. Don't get overwhelmed with this example, as you will read more about the messaging APIs in the following topics in this chapter.

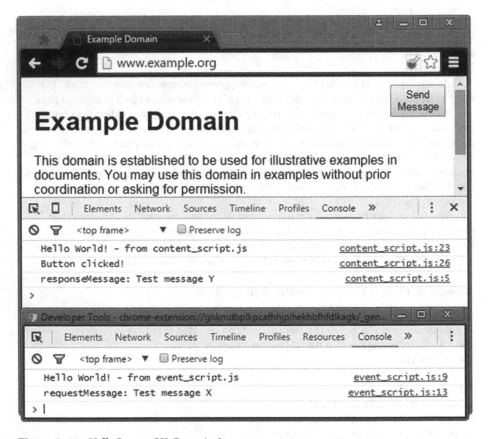

Figure 3-14. *HelloContentUI: Page-Action component*

Messaging for Communication

By now you have tried different sscripting components to accomplish different purposes. But there are scenarios where a single type of scripting component is not sufficient to get the job done—for example, consider the HelloContentUI extension discussed previously. In that extension, you needed the content script and the event script (i.e., the extension runtime) to communicate with each other in order to show the Page-Action component.

In addition to this, apart from the scripting components belonging to an extension, normal (external) web pages may also want to interact with an extension. So, in all, there are four types of scripts that can communicate with each other—content scripts, popup scripts, event scripts (or background scripts), and web page scripts (belonging to external web pages that need to interact with an extension).

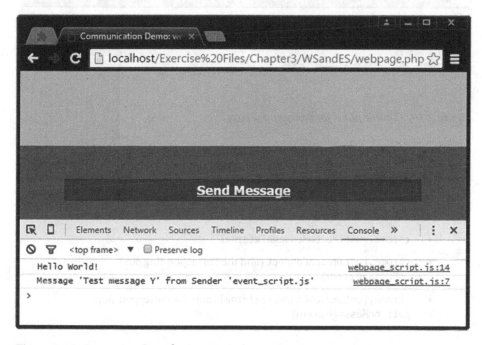

Figure 3-15. Inspecting the web page: Console panel

APIs and Events

Now we can talk about the actual messaging APIs that are used for communication between different scripting components. These APIs are from the standard JavaScript APIs and the Extensions framework. The messaging API provided by the standard JavaScript APIs includes the window.postMessage method. Similarly, the messaging APIs provided by the Extensions framework includes the following methods:

- chrome.runtime.sendMessage

- chrome.runtime.connect (and the corresponding port.
  postMessage method)

- chrome.tabs.sendMessage

- chrome.tabs.connect (and the corresponding port.postMessage
  method)

95

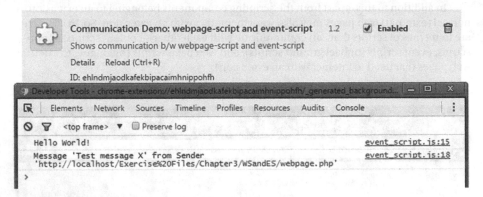

Figure 3-16. *Console panel for background page*

The corresponding event for the messaging API in the standard JavaScript APIs includes the message event. And similarly, the corresponding events for the messaging APIs in the Extensions framework include the following events. Now that you have an overview of messaging, let's try different examples to understand these concepts more clearly.

- `chrome.runtime.onMessage`

- `chrome.runtime.onMessageExternal`

- `chrome.runtime.onConnect` (and the corresponding `port.onMessage` event)

- `chrome.runtime.onConnectExternal` (and the corresponding `port.onMessage` event)

Web Page Scripts and Event Scripts

The basic idea here is to allow an external web page to communicate with the extension runtime. In the Chrome browser, all web pages (except the Extensions Management page) have access to the `chrome.runtime.sendMessage` method, which is used to send messages to the extension runtime. This method takes the following parameters.

- `extensionID`

- `message`

- `responseCallback`

As seen in Listing 3-9, clicking the button `send_message` leads to the `chrome.runtime.sendMessage(extensionID,message,responseCallback)` call. Note that `extensionID` is the ID of the extension to send the message to. This ID can be viewed from the Extensions Management page (see Figure 3-16). Also note that this ID will change upon loading the extension every time a change is made in the extension contents or in the extension folder's location. Moreover, the modifications to `manifest.json` (or any other file in the extension's folder) will only take effect upon reinstalling or reloading the extension!

■ **Note** For the WSandES extension, the contents of the folder WebServer have been served from my local HTTP server to give a demonstration that is close to the real-world scenario, where your extension might be attempting to listen for messages from external web pages (visited on the Chrome browser).

Also note that the served web page has a .php suffix but contains plain HTML code. For this reason, it can be opened directly in the Chrome browser as a local file web page (i.e., using the file:// scheme).

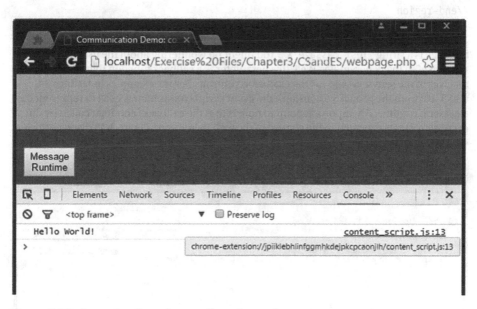

Figure 3-17. *Inspecting the web page: Console panel*

Listing 3-9. Chapter3/WSandES/WebServer/webpage_script.js

```
//region {variables and functions}
//Note this from the extensions page
var extensionID = "lconbphjmfkpdopdnadkdfiiflajajgg";
var sendMessageButtonID = "send_message";
var greeting = "Hello World!";
var message = "Test message X";
function responseCallback(responseObject) {
    console.log("Message '" +
        responseObject.message + "' from Sender '" +
        responseObject.sender + "'"
    );
```

```
}
//end-region

//region {calls}
console.log(greeting);
document.addEventListener("DOMContentLoaded",function(dcle) {
    var buttonID = document.getElementById(sendMessageButtonID);
    buttonID.addEventListener("click",function(ce) {
        //This message will be intercepted by event_script.js
        chrome.runtime.sendMessage(extensionID,message,responseCallback);
    });
});
//end-region
```

The message parameter in sendMessage is the message to send. In this case, the message is a string "Test message X". You might be wondering about the use of the responseCallback parameter. Well, this parameter is a callback function that is used by the receiver of the sent message, i.e. the extension runtime. For the examples in Listings 3-9 and 3-10 (from the WSandES extension), the event script component is used to represent the extension runtime. An important point to note is that the callback (although called by the event script) gets executed in the context of the web page script. Figure 3-15 displays the log corresponding to the sendResponse(responseObject) call in the event script.

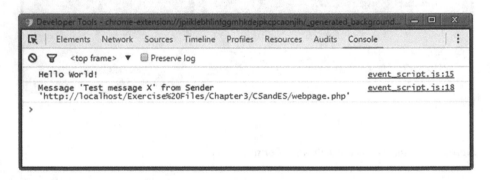

Figure 3-18. *Console panel for background page*

Listening to the Event

As shown in Listing 3-10, the listener function for the chrome.runtime.onMessageExternal event is used to handle the incoming message from the external web page. The listener function for the onMessageExternal event takes three parameters—message, sender, and sendResponse. As discussed, sendResponse is the callback that gets executed in the context of the web page script. Note the passed argument called responseObject.

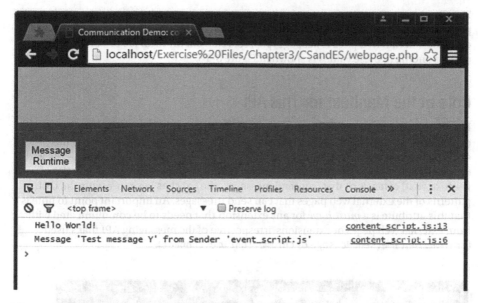

Figure 3-19. *Inspecting the web page: Console panel*

Listing 3-10. Chapter3/WSandES/event_script.js

```
//region {variables and functions}
var greeting = "Hello World!";
var responseObject = {
    message : "Test message Y",
    sender : "event_script.js"
};
function GetFormattedMessageString(message,sender) {
    return "Message '" + message + "' from Sender '" + sender.url + "'";
}
//end-region

//region {calls}
console.log(greeting);
chrome.runtime.onMessageExternal.addListener(
    function(message,sender,sendResponse) {
        //Will get called from the script where sendResponse is defined
        sendResponse(responseObject);
        console.log(GetFormattedMessageString(message,sender));
    }
);
//end-region
```

The `message` parameter contains the passed message. And similarly, the `sender` parameter contains the URL of the external web page that sent the message. In this case, the external web page is `webpage.php`, served from my local HTTP server. The log corresponding to these values is shown in Figure 3-16.

Role of the Manifest for This API

For an extension to be able to receive messages from external web pages (or other extensions), an important addition is required in the manifest. This addition is the `externally_connectable` manifest attribute. This attribute contains two keys—`ids` and `matches`. Both of these keys take array values. While the `ids` key represents the IDs of the (external) extensions that can send messages, the `matches` key represents the URL patterns of the external web pages that can send messages. An important point to note is that this attribute is a *must-have* for any extension that needs to be communicated with from external web pages or extensions, irrespective of the messaging API that's used (`chrome.runtime.sendMessage` or `chrome.runtime.connect`).

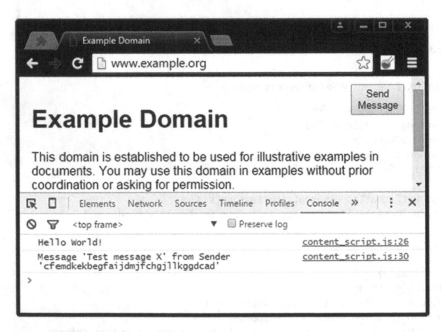

Figure 3-20. *Inspecting the web page: Console panel*

For the WSandES extension (provided in Chapter 3's Exercise Files folder), the externally_connectable attribute is defined the following way. This is done so as to only allow web pages served from the localhost to send messages to the extension runtime.

```
"externally_connectable" : {
    //Extension and app IDs. If this field is not specified, no
    //extensions or apps can communicate.
    //"ids" : [], //To match all extensions and apps, specify only "*"
    //Allowed webpages
    "matches" : ["*://localhost/*"]
}
```

Using Long-Lived Connections

The messaging example that was demonstrated in this topic involved a single message and response. Sometimes it is useful to have a conversation that lasts longer than that. To facilitate this purpose, the Extensions framework provides the chrome.runtime.connect method. Note that apart from the web page script, this method is also available to other scripts, including to content script and popup script.

■ **Note**   Obviously, the event script can also use the chrome.runtime.connect method. But you will rarely find this application. However, you will definitely find a frequent use of the chrome.runtime.onConnect (or the chrome.runtime.onConnectExternal) event with its listener function in the event script. The connect method will mainly be used from within the event script to communicate with another extension. The same holds true for the sendMessage method. You can read more about cross-extension messaging at https:// developer.chrome.com/extensions/messaging#external.

This method takes the extensionID as its first parameter. This is the ID of the extension you need to connect to for a long-lived connection. The second parameter is an object, which can be used to provide additional information about the connection—for example, {"name" : "connection1"}. Note that this method returns a port object. The port.postMessage method is used to send message to the extension runtime. The code discussed so far (for the web page script) is summarized as following.

```
var port = chrome.runtime.connect("...",{"name" : "connection1"});
port.onMessage.addListener(function(message) {
    console.log(message);
});
port.postMessage("Test message X");
```

Next, on the receiving end (i.e., the extension runtime represented using an event script), the listener function for the chrome.runtime.onConnectExternal event (or the chrome.runtime.onConnect event, for connection made from within the extension) also receives the port object. Note that in this case—i.e., for connection between a web page script and event script—the onConnectExternal event needs to be used, because it gets fired when a connection is made from an external web page (or extension).

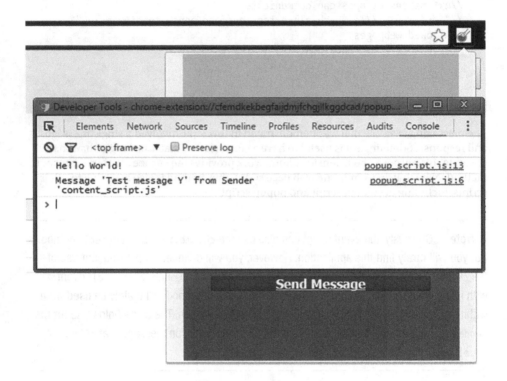

Figure 3-21. *Inspecting the popup: Console panel*

Finally, using the listener function for the port.onMessage event (available to both ends of the connection), you can listen for the incoming messages. Note that since each end has access to the port object, they can do the both. That means they can send as well as receive messages through the established connection (via the port). The code discussed so far (for the event script) is summarized as following:

```
chrome.runtime.onConnectExternal.addListener(function(port) {
    //if(port.name == "connection1")
    port.onMessage.addListener(function(message) {
        console.log(message); //Test message X
        port.postMessage("Test message Y");
    });
});
```

Content Scripts and Event Scripts

Recall that the content script component does not represent the extension runtime. But it does have access to the following APIs in the Extensions framework—extension, i18n, runtime, and storage. And in the runtime API, the content script component has access to connect and sendMessage methods. And access to events runtime.onConnect (including the corresponding port.onMessage event) and runtime.onMessage.

Note that the content script component does not have access to the runtime. onMessageExternal and runtime.onConnectExternal events. For this reason, it cannot rely on the runtime APIs to communicate with the web page scripts. Instead, it needs to listen for the message event provided by the standard JavaScript APIs to do so. First let's take a look at how content scripts can communicate with the extension runtime, and then in the following topics, you will learn how popup scripts and web page scripts can communicate with a content script.

For this purpose, evaluate Listings 3-11 to 3-13 from the CSandES extension. Note from the manifest file (Listing 3-13) that this extension injects content scripts into the visited web pages belonging to the localhost. This is specified using the "*://localhost/*" string in the matches array. The corresponding script that gets injected is content_script.js (see Figures 3-17 and 3-19). Listing 3-11 contains the code from this script.

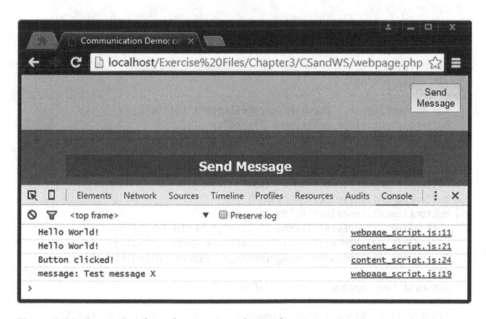

Figure 3-22. *Inspecting the web page: Console panel*

> ■ **Note** For popup scripts and event scripts to be able to communicate with the content scripts, the `chrome.runtime.sendMessage` method cannot be used. Instead, the `chrome.tabs.sendMessage` (or `chrome.tabs.connect`) method needs to be used. For the `chrome.tabs.sendMessage` method, the corresponding event remains the same—i.e., `chrome.runtime.onMessage` (and similarly the event `chrome.runtime.onConnect` for the `chrome.tabs.connect` method).

Listing 3-11. Chapter3/CSandES/content_script.js

```
//region {variables and functions}
var sendMessageButtonID = "send_message";
var greeting = "Hello World!";
var message = "Test message X";
function responseCallback(responseObject) {
    console.log("Message '" + responseObject.message +
        "' from Sender '" + responseObject.sender + "'"
    );
}
//end-region

//region {calls}
console.log(greeting);
(function(){
    var buttonElement = document.createElement("button");
    buttonElement.style.position = "fixed";
    buttonElement.style.display = "block";
    buttonElement.style.width = "70px";
    buttonElement.style.height = "40px";
    buttonElement.style.bottom = "10px";
    buttonElement.style.left = "10px";
    buttonElement.innerText = "Message Runtime";
    buttonElement.addEventListener("click",function(ce) {
        //This message will be intercepted by event_script.js
        chrome.runtime.sendMessage(message,responseCallback);
    });
    document.body.appendChild(buttonElement);
    /*
    //var port = chrome.runtime.connect("...",{"name":"connection1"});
    var port = chrome.runtime.connect({"name":"connection1"});
    port.onMessage.addListener(function(message){console.log(message);});
    port.postMessage("...");
    */
})();
//end-region
```

104

As shown in Listing 3-11, as soon as the content script gets injected, it appends a button element into the visited web page. This element has a listener function attached to its `click` event. To send messages to the extension runtime, it calls the `chrome.runtime.sendMessage` method. Note that compared to the previous use of this method (in Listing 3-9), here, the `extensionID` parameter is not used. This is because it is an optional parameter. Since messaging is being performed within the extension, the `extensionID` parameter defaults to the ID of the current extension. Also note that, similar to how the `sendMessage` method has been used, you can also use the `connect` method. Once again, the first parameter of the connect method can also be omitted.

Listing 3-12. Chapter3/CSandES/event_script.js

```
//region {variables and functions}
var greeting = "Hello World!";
var responseObject = {
    message : "Test message Y",
    sender : "event_script.js"
};
function GetFormattedMessageString(message,sender) {
    return "Message '" + message + "' from Sender '" + sender.url + "'";
}
//end-region

//region {calls}
console.log(greeting);
chrome.runtime.onMessage.addListener(function(message,sender,sendResponse) {
    //Will get called from the script where sendResponse is defined
    sendResponse(responseObject);
    console.log(GetFormattedMessageString(message,sender));
});
/*
chrome.runtime.onConnect.addListener(function(port) {
    port.onMessage.addListener(function(message){console.log(message);});
    port.postMessage("...");
});
*/
//end-region
```

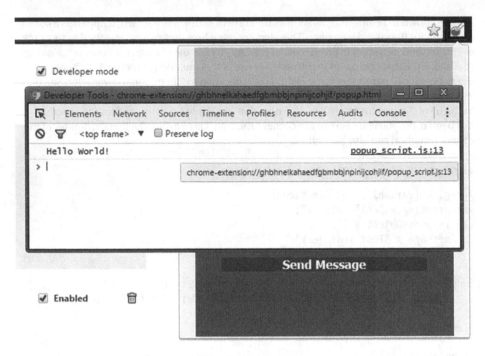

Figure 3-23. Inspecting the popup: PSandES extension

Listing 3-12 contains the corresponding code for the event script. Note that compared to the previous example (see Listing 3-10), the onMessageExternal event is not used here. Instead the onMessage event is used, since messaging is being performed within the extension. If a long-lived connection were to be used (using the chrome.runtime.connect method; see Listing 3-11), the code for the event script would need a listener function for the chrome.runtime.onConnect event. This has been displayed in the commented-out section in Listing 3-12. Figure 3-18 contains the log corresponding to the event script.

Listing 3-13. Chapter3/CSandES/manifest.json

```
{
    "manifest_version" : 2,
    "name" : "Communication Demo: content-script and event-script",
    "description" : "Shows communication b/w content-script and
    event-script",
    "version" : "1.2",
    "background" : {
        "scripts" : ["event_script.js"],
        "persistent" : false
    },
    "content_scripts" : [
```

```
{
    "matches" : ["*://localhost/*"],
    "js" : ["content_script.js"]
    }
  ]
}
```

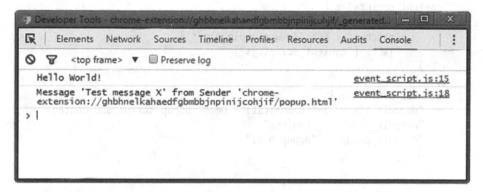

Figure 3-24. Console panel for background page

Popup Scripts and Content Scripts

Now, let's take a look at how a popup script can communicate with the content script. To demonstrate this, the Exercise Files folder contains the PSandCS extension. Listings 3-14 to 3-16 contain the relevant code from this extension. You can load this extension in your browser for testing. Figures 3-20 and 3-21 contain the logs from the content script and the popup script (respectively) from this extension.

■ **Note**   If the extension's Browser-Action does not contain a popup, an event script can be used to provide a listener function for the chrome.browserAction.onClicked event. Using this listener function, you can call the chrome.tabs.sendMessage (or chrome.tabs. connect) method. This approach does not require use of the tabs API, since the listener function receives the active tab as its argument. This will still require the activeTab permission, in order to interact with the content of the active tab—for example, via the chrome.tabs.executeScript method.

As you can see from the manifest file (Listing 3-14), this extension injects content scripts into the visited web pages belonging to the example.org host. Note the use of the browser_action attribute, along with its popup component. The popup contains a clickable element (see Figure 3-21)—"Send Message" with an ID of send_message. A listener function is attached to the click event on this element. Listing 3-15 contains the corresponding code for the listener function.

Listing 3-14. Chapter3/PSandCS/manifest.json

```
{
    "manifest_version" : 2,
    "name" : "Communication Demo: popup-script and content-script",
    "description" : "Shows communication b/w popup-script and content-script",
    "version" : "1.2",
    "content_scripts" : [
        {
            "matches" : ["*://www.example.org/*"],
            "js" : ["content_script.js"]
        }
    ],
    "browser_action" : {
        "default_title" : "Communication Demo: popup-script and content...",
        "default_icon" : "icon.png",
        "default_popup" : "popup.html"
    }
}
```

In Listing 3-15, note the use of chrome.tabs.query method to get the (currently) active tab. As described earlier, the chrome.tabs.sendMessage method is used to send message to the content script. This method takes the following parameters.

- tabID

- message

- responseCallback

The tabID is the ID of the tab to send messages to. The message parameter is the message to send. In this case, it is a string "Test message X". And similar to the previously discussed extensions, responseCallback is a callback function that is used by the receiver of the sent message.

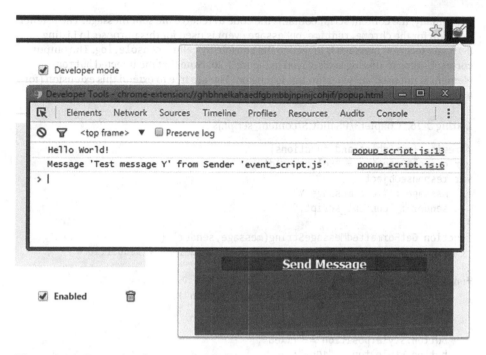

Figure 3-25. *Inspecting the popup: PSandES extension*

Listing 3-15. Chapter3/PSandCS/popup_script.js

```
//region {variables and functions}
var sendMessageButtonID = "send_message";
var greeting = "Hello World!";
var message = "Test message X";
function responseCallback(responseObject) {
    console.log("Message '" + responseObject.message +
    "' from Sender '" + responseObject.sender + "'");
}
//end-region

//region {calls}
console.log(greeting);
document.addEventListener("DOMContentLoaded",function(dcle){
    var buttonID = document.getElementById(sendMessageButtonID);
    buttonID.addEventListener("click",function(ce) {
        chrome.tabs.query({"active":true},function(tabs) {
            chrome.tabs.sendMessage(tabs[0].id,message,responseCallback);
        });
    });
});
//end-region
```

109

Finally, the content script contains the code to receive the sent message. The listener function for the chrome.runtime.onMessage event is used for this purpose. In Listing 3-16, the received message is logged to the console by calling console.log. The output corresponding to this log is displayed in Figure 3-20. Note that the injected button element is not used anywhere in this extension. You are free to extend this extension (for experimentation, etc.) by making use of the available code.

Listing 3-16. Chapter3/PSandCS/content_script.js

```javascript
//region {variables and functions}
var consoleGreeting = "Hello World!";
var responseObject = {
    message : "Test message Y",
    sender : "content_script.js"
};
function GetFormattedMessageString(message,sender) {
    return "Message '" + message + "' from Sender '" + sender.id + "'";
}
function createButton() {
    var button = document.createElement("button");
    button.style.width = "70px";
    button.style.height = "40px";
    button.style.position = "fixed";
    button.style.top = "10px";
    button.style.right = "10px";
    button.innerText = "Send Message";
    document.body.appendChild(button);
    return button;
}
//end-region

//region {calls}
console.log(consoleGreeting);
var button = createButton();
chrome.runtime.onMessage.addListener(function(message,sender,sendResponse) {
    //Will get called from the script where sendResponse is defined
    sendResponse(responseObject);
    console.log(GetFormattedMessageString(message,sender));
});
//end-region
```

Using a Long-lived Connection

To create a long-lived connection to communicate with the content script, the chrome.tabs.connect method can be used. This method takes the ID of the tab (to connect to) as its only parameter. The corresponding chrome.runtime.onConnect event is fired in each content script running in the specified tab for the current extension.

Once again, since both ends of the connection have access to the port object – port.postMessage method and the corresponding port.onMessage event can be used for communication. This is similar to the way it was done in the topic "Web Page Scripts and Event Scripts".

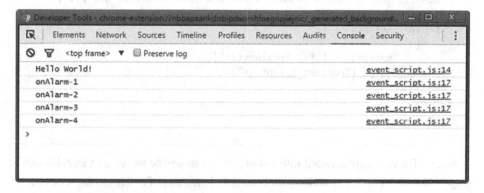

Figure 3-26. *API demos: Alarms API*

Content Scripts and Web Page Scripts

As described earlier, content scripts do not have access to the runtime.onMessageExternal and runtime.onConnectExternal events. For this reason, they cannot rely on the runtime APIs to communicate with the web page scripts. Instead, they need to listen for the message event provided by the standard JavaScript APIs to do so. For this purpose, let's examine the CSandWS extension provided in the Exercise Files folder of this chapter. Listings 3-17 to 3-19 contain the relevant code from this extension.

As seen in the manifest file for this extension, using the content_scripts attribute, a content script is injected into the visited web pages belonging to the localhost. Note that for the purpose demonstrated by this extension, an HTTP server is not necessary to serve the external web pages. But it has been done so to display secure use of the window.postMessage method and the message event. If the content script were to be injected in a local file web page, the target origin (i.e., URL or URI of the window that would receive the messages) in the postMessage method would need to be specified as *. This is strongly discouraged for security reasons, as it would allow messages from all hosts.

■ **Note**   A local file in this context is a file accessed in the browser using the file:// scheme. An example of a local file web page is file:///F:/Exercise%20Files/somefile.html. This is different from a web page served from the localhost that uses http:// or https:// schemes.

Listing 3-17. Chapter3/CSandWS/manifest.json

```json
{
    "manifest_version" : 2,
    "name" : "Communication Demo: content-script and webpage-script",
    "description" : "Shows communication b/w content-script and ...",
    "version" : "1.2",
    "content_scripts" : [
        {
            "matches" : ["*://localhost/*"],
            "js" : ["content_script.js"]
        }
    ]
}
```

■ **Note** The web page provided with this extension can also be served as a local file web page. Although it has a .php suffix, it contains plain HTML code. For this reason, it can be opened directly in the Chrome browser (i.e., as a local file web page using the file:// scheme).

Listing 3-18 contains the code from the injected content script. The button variable refers the created button element—Send Message. This element can be seen at the top-right of Figure 3-22. Note that this button element has a listener function associated with its click event. Upon clicking this element, the listener function first logs the "Button clicked!" string to the console. Then it calls the postMessage method—window.postMessage(message,targetOrigin).

Quite obviously, message argument is the message to send. And as described, targetOrigin is the URL or URI of the window that will receive the messages. Note that in this case, targetOrigin points to the origin of the current window: var targetOrigin = window.location.origin. Also note that all the following values for targetOrigin are invalid: "file://", "file://*", "", and null. To use the messaging API in a local file web page, postMessage needs be called as window.postMessage(message,"*").

■ **Note** To inject content scripts into local file web pages, you need to define the matches attribute as "matches" : ["file://*"].

Regardless of the scheme the web page is served with (i.e., http:// or https:// versus file://), to receive a sent message, a listener function for the message event is required to be created, as shown in the window.addEventListener("message",function(me){/**/}) line. The same has been done in Listing 3-19. The log corresponding to its listener function can be seen in Figure 3-22. Note that the event that gets passed to this listener function has a data property that can be used to access the string or object that was sent by the postMessage method.

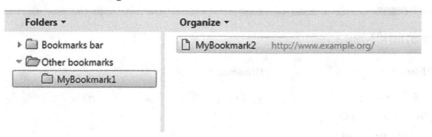

Figure 3-27. *API demos: Bookmarks API*

Listing 3-18. Chapter3/CSandWS/content_script.js

```
//region {variables and functions}
var consoleGreeting = "Hello World!";
var targetOrigin = window.location.origin;
var message = "Test message X";
function createButton() {
    var button = document.createElement("button");
    button.style.width = "70px";
    button.style.height = "40px";
    button.style.position = "fixed";
    button.style.top = "10px";
    button.style.right = "10px";
    button.innerText = "Send Message";
    document.body.appendChild(button);
    return button;
}
//end-region

//region {calls}
console.log(consoleGreeting);
var button = createButton();
button.addEventListener("click",function() {
    console.log("Button clicked!");
    window.postMessage(message,targetOrigin);
});
/*
window.addEventListener("message",function(me) {
    console.log("message: " + me.data);
});
*/
//end-region
```

113

For this extension, messaging was initiated from the content script. In a similar way you can extend this extension to initiate messaging from the web page script. You can use the existing listener function for the click event in the web page script to do so. To handle the send message, the content script should contain the corresponding listener function.

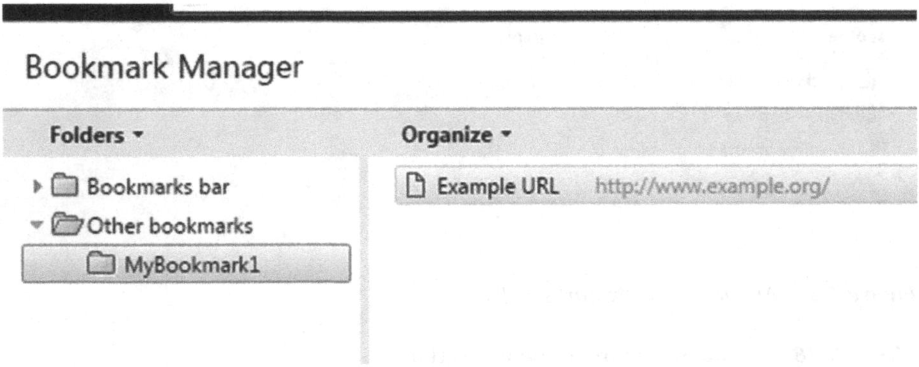

Bookmark Manager

Folders ▾	Organize ▾
▶ 📁 Bookmarks bar	🗋 Example URL http://www.example.org/
▾ 📂 Other bookmarks	
📁 MyBookmark1	

Figure 3-28. *API demos: Bookmarks API*

Listing 3-19. Chapter3/CSandWS/WebServer/webpage_script.js

```javascript
//region {variables and functions}
var sendMessageButtonID = "send_message";
var greeting = "Hello World!";
//var targetOrigin = window.location.origin;
//var message = "Test message Y";
//end-region

//region {calls}
console.log(greeting);
document.addEventListener("DOMContentLoaded",function(dcle) {
    var buttonID = document.getElementById(sendMessageButtonID);
    buttonID.addEventListener("click",function(ce) {
        //window.postMessage(message,targetOrigin);
    });
});
window.addEventListener("message",function(me) {
    console.log("message: " + me.data);
});
//end-region
```

Popup Scripts and Event Scripts

Now let's see how a popup script can communicate with the event script. Although both these components represent the extension runtime, they exist as different scripting components in the extensions architecture. This is why there is a need for communication between these two scripting components. Having these components communicate with each other is a lot easier than it is for other components.

Listing 3-20. Chapter3/PSandES/manifest.json

```
{
    "manifest_version" : 2,
    "name" : "Communication Demo: popup-script and event-script",
    "description" : "Shows communication b/w popup-script and event-script",
    "version" : "1.2",
    "browser_action" : {
        "default_title" : "Communication Demo: popup-script and event-
        script",
        "default_icon" : "icon.png",
        "default_popup" : "popup.html"
    },
    "background" : {
        "scripts" : ["event_script.js"],
        "persistent" : false
    }
}
```

Since a popup script is being used, it is obvious that the extension will need a Browser-Action or Page-Action component with a popup. This can be seen in Listing 3-20, from the PSandES extension (in Chapter 3's Exercise Files folder). To use an event script, the background attribute has been defined in the manifest. Listing 3-22 contains the code for the corresponding event script component.

Listing 3-21. Chapter3/PSandES/popup_script.js

```
//region {variables and functions}
var sendMessageButtonID = "send_message";
var greeting = "Hello World!";
var message = "Test message X";
function responseCallback(responseObject) {
    console.log("Message '" + responseObject.message +
    "' from Sender '" + responseObject.sender + "'");
}
//end-region
```

```
//region {calls}
console.log(greeting);
document.addEventListener("DOMContentLoaded",function(dcle){
    var buttonID = document.getElementById(sendMessageButtonID);
    buttonID.addEventListener("click",function(ce) {
        //This message will be intercepted by event_script.js
        chrome.runtime.sendMessage(message,responseCallback);
    });
});
//end-region
```

As discussed in the previous examples, to send a message to the event script, the following call needs to be made: chrome.runtime.sendMessage(message,response Callback). As you know already, the message parameter is the message to send. The responseCallback is a callback function that is used by the receiver of the sent message. Note that Listing 3-21 contains the code from the popup script used in the PSandES extension. Figures 3-23 and 3-25 display the logs from the popup script.

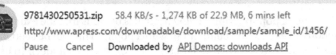

Figure 3-29. *API demos: Downloads API*

Listing 3-22. Chapter3/PSandES/event_script.js

```
//region {variables and functions}
var greeting = "Hello World!";
var responseObject = {
    message : "Test message Y",
    sender : "event_script.js"
};
function GetFormattedMessageString(message,sender) {
    return "Message '" + message + "' from Sender '" + sender.url + "'";
}
//end-region
```

```
//region {calls}
console.log(greeting);
chrome.runtime.onMessage.addListener(function(message,sender,sendResponse) {
    //Will get called from the script where sendResponse is defined
    sendResponse(responseObject);
    console.log(GetFormattedMessageString(message,sender));
});
//end-region
```

Finally, to receive the sent message, the event script provides the listener function for the chrome.runtime.onMessage event. The log corresponding to this function is shown in Figure 3-24. Note the sendResponse callback and the passed argument responseObject, which is logged to the console in the context of the popup script (see Figure 3-25).

Google Chrome Extensions APIs

The Google Chrome Extensions framework provides extensions with many special-purpose APIs that allow you to access amazing features of the Chrome browser. These APIs provide access to almost every feature available in the Chrome browser! A lot of APIs have already been discussed, although they were described in a different context. For example, the following APIs were described as input components: chrome.omnibox, chrome.contextMenus, chrome.commands, chrome.pageAction, and chrome.browserAction. This section looks at the following APIs:

- alarms
- bookmarks
- downloads
- history
- notifications
- storage
- tabs

■ **Note** Extensions can still use all the standard APIs (also known as the standard JavaScript APIs) that the browser provides to web pages. These are the same core JavaScript and Document Object Model (DOM) APIs that you are already familiar with. Additionally, XMLHttpRequest (XHR) APIs, HTML5 APIs, WebKit APIs (for CSS animations, filters, etc.), and V8 APIs (such as JSON) are supported!

In addition to these APIs from the Extensions framework, this section also covers the XHR API from the standard JavaScript APIs. Other APIs that are not discussed here—but that you can read about in the online documentation at `https://developer.chrome.com/extensions/api_index`—include the following:

- `contentSettings`
- `cookies`
- `desktopCapture`
- `extension`
- `management`
- `system.cpu`
- `system.memory`
- `webstore`
- `windows`

Declare Permissions

To use most `chrome.*` APIs, your extension (or app) must declare its intent in the `permissions` field of the manifest. Every such permission in the `permissions` field can be one of a list of known strings (such as "`alarms`", "`storage`", "`tabs`", etc.—see the following list containing all permission strings) or a *match pattern* that gives access to one or more hosts. In all the examples discussed until this point, you haven't seen a *match pattern* in the `permissions` field of the manifest. This is because such use is only required alongside the XHR API (more about it later in this section).

An Example of Permissions

The following code snippet is an example of the `permissions` part of a manifest file. As you might have guessed by looking at this code, the "`alarms`", "`tabs`", and "`bookmarks`" permission strings are required to access the alarms, tabs, and bookmarks APIs (respectively). And unlike these permission strings, the remaining two permission strings (i.e., the URLs) are required to talk to remote hosts outside of the extension's origin (via XHR).

```
"permissions" : [
    "alarms", //Extensions-API permission
    "tabs", //Extensions-API permission
    "bookmarks", //Extensions-API permission
    "http://www.blogger.com/", //XHR permission
    "http://*.google.com/" //XHR permission
],
```

APIs Requiring Permissions

The documentation corresponding to an API in the Google Chrome Extensions framework specifies the need for a permission string (if any). In addition to this, if an API requires you to declare a permission string in the manifest, then its documentation tells you how to do so. For example, the Alarms API documentation—found at https://developer.chrome. com/extensions/alarms—shows you how to declare the alarms permission.

- activeTab
- alarms
- audioModem
- background
- bookmarks
- browsingData
- clipboardRead
- clipboardWrite
- contentSettings
- contextMenus
- cookies
- copresence
- debugger
- declarativeContent
- declarativeWebRequest
- desktopCapture
- dns
- documentScan
- downloads
- enterprise.platformKeys
- experimental
- fileBrowserHandler
- fileSystemProvider
- fontSettings
- gcm
- geolocation

- history
- identity
- idle
- idltest
- location
- management
- nativeMessaging
- networking.config
- notificationProvider
- notifications
- pageCapture
- platformKeys
- power
- printerProvider
- privacy
- processes
- proxy
- sessions
- signedInDevices
- storage
- system.cpu
- system.display
- system.memory
- system.storage
- tabCapture
- tabs
- topSites
- tts
- ttsEngine
- unlimitedStorage
- vpnProvider

- `wallpaper`
- `webNavigation`
- `webRequest`
- `webRequestBlocking`

■ **Note** Permissions help to limit damage if your extension or app is compromised by malware. Some of the permissions are also displayed to users, before installation of the extension (or app), as a warning. You can read more about these warnings at `https://developer.chrome.com/extensions/permission_warnings`.

Optional Permissions

There are two types of permissions—*required permissions* and *optional permissions*. The permissions you've dealt with so far are required permissions. Optional permissions are permissions that can be requested at runtime, rather than install time. Users understand why the permissions are needed and grant only those that are necessary. Though optional permissions are more informative for users, they are not described here due to their complexity. You can read more about them at `https://developer.chrome.com/extensions/permissions`.

Alarms API

The alarms API (i.e., the `chrome.alarms` API) is used to schedule code to run periodically or at a specified time in the future. It uses the `alarms` permission. Listing 3-23 contains the code from the `AlarmsAPI` extension, provided in Chapter 3's `Exercise Files` folder.

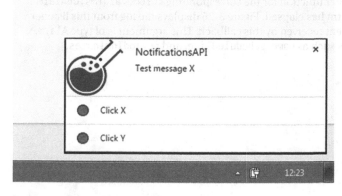

Figure 3-30. *API demos: Notifications API*

To create an alarm, use the `chrome.alarms.create` method. This method takes two parameters—`alarmName` (of type `string`) and `alarmInfo` (of type `object`). The `alarmInfo` object describes when the alarm should fire. The initial time must be specified by either when or `delayInMinutes` (but not both).

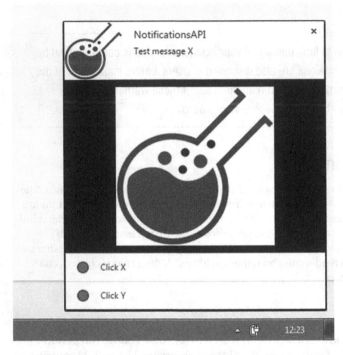

Figure 3-31. *API demos: Notifications API*

If `periodInMinutes` is set, the alarm will repeat every `periodInMinutes` minutes after the initial event. The listener function for the corresponding `chrome.alarms.onAlarm` event is fired when an alarm has elapsed. Figure 3-26 displays the log from this listener function. Note the argument received by this callback. This argument is of type `Alarm`, which contains properties such as `name`, `scheduledTime`, and `periodInMinutes`.

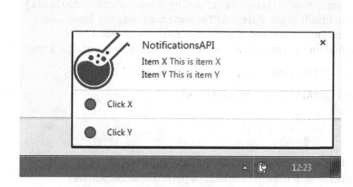

Figure 3-32. API demos: Notifications API

■ **Note**   While debugging an extension, which is loaded unpacked, there's no limit to how often the alarm can fire. For all other cases, alarms with intervals of less than one minute will not be honored and will cause a warning. Refer back to the topic "Loading the Extension Folder" (from Chapter 1) to remind yourself of the basics of extension loading.

Listing 3-23. Chapter3/AlarmsAPI/event_script.js

```
//region {variables and functions}
var greeting = "Hello World!";
var count = 0;
var alarmName = "testAlarm";
var alarmInfo = {
    when : Date.now() + 6000,
    periodInMinutes : 1 //Repeatedly fire after every 1 minute
};
//end-region

//region {calls}
console.log(greeting);
chrome.alarms.clearAll();
chrome.alarms.onAlarm.addListener(function(alarm) {
    console.log("onAlarm-" + ++count);
});
chrome.alarms.create(alarmName,alarmInfo);
//end-region
```

In Listing 3-23, the chrome.alarms.clearAll method is used to clear all alarms. To clear a specific alarm, use the chrome.alarms.clear(string name, function callback) method. Other important methods in the alarms API include the following. Here, note that the callback function for the get method receives an argument of type Alarm, whereas the callback function for the getAll method receives an argument of type array.

- chrome.alarms.get(string name, function callback)

- chrome.alarms.getAll(function callback)

Bookmarks API

The bookmarks API (i.e., the chrome.bookmarks API) is used to create, organize, and otherwise manipulate bookmarks. It uses the bookmarks permission. Bookmarks are organized in a tree, where each node in the tree is either a bookmark or a folder. Each node in the tree is represented by a bookmarks.BookmarkTreeNode object. BookmarkTreeNode properties are used throughout the chrome.bookmarks API. For example, when you call chrome.bookmarks.create, you pass in the new node's parent (parentId), and optionally, the node's title and url properties. To read about the complete list of properties a node can have, refer to https://developer.chrome.com/extensions/bookmarks#type-BookmarkTreeNode.

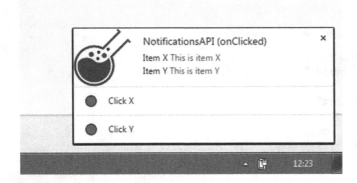

Figure 3-33. *API demos: Notifications API*

Note that if a node is a folder, it has the following properties—id, parentId, children, and title. And if it's a bookmark, it has the following properties—id, parentId, title, and url. Moreover, the root node for the bookmarks tree does not have any parent, so there isn't any parentId. It has the following two special folders as its children—Bookmarks Bar and Other Bookmarks.

■ **Note** You cannot use this API to add or remove entries in the root node. You also cannot rename, move, or remove the special Bookmarks Bar and Other Bookmarks folders.

Creating a Bookmark

To create a bookmark, use the chrome.bookmarks.create method. This method takes two parameters—bookmark (of type object) and callback (of type function). Using the properties defined in the bookmark object—parentId, title, and url—you can create a bookmark or a folder. Note that if url is null or missing, the created bookmark will be a folder. The callback function receives an argument of type BookmarkTreeNode.

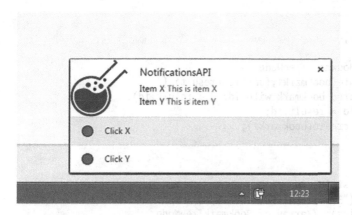

Figure 3-34. *API demos: Notifications API*

Listing 3-24 contains the corresponding code snippet, where, using the bookmark1 object, first a folder is created, and then a bookmark is created inside this folder. This is done using the result.id value in the callback function. Also see Figure 3-27, which contains the created folder and bookmark. An interesting thing to note is that the id of the created folder (highlighted in blue) is 373, as can be seen from the URL chrome://bookmarks/#373. You can examine this by using the chrome.bookmarks.get method, as seen in Listing 3-24. This method takes a string id, or an array of these, along with a callback function as its parameters. The callback function receives a results argument, which is an array of BookmarkTreeNode objects.

Listing 3-24. Chapter3/BookmarksAPI/event_script.js

```
//region {variables and functions}
var greeting = "Hello World!";
var bookmark1 = {
    title : "MyBookmark1",
    //If url is null or missing, created bookmark will be a folder
    url : ""
};
var bookmark2 = {
    title : "MyBookmark2",
    url : "http://www.example.org"
```

```
};
var queryObject = {
    query : "",
    url : "",
    title : "chrome extensions"
};
var queryString = "example url";
//end-region

//region {calls}
console.log(greeting);
/*
//result is of type BookmarkTreeNode
chrome.bookmarks.create(bookmark1,function(result) {
    console.log("Created bookmark with id: " + result.id);
    bookmark2.parentId = result.id;
    chrome.bookmarks.create(bookmark2);
});
*/
/*
//string or array of string id
chrome.bookmarks.get("373",function(results) {
    console.log(results); //array of BookmarkTreeNode
});
*/
/*
//only title and url are supported
chrome.bookmarks.update("374",{"title":"Example URL"});
*/
//string or object query
chrome.bookmarks.search(queryString,function(results) {
    console.log(results); //array of BookmarkTreeNode
});
//end-region
```

Updating a Bookmark

A bookmark (or a folder) can also be updated. The specific properties that are allowed to be updated include title and url. Note that url is only valid for a bookmark that is not a folder. To update a bookmark, call the chrome.bookmarks.update method. This method takes the following parameters—id (of type string), changes (of type object), and callback (of type function).

Note the passed string id in the update method in Listing 3-24. This id corresponds to the bookmark shown in Figure 3-27 (i.e., MyBookmark2). Figure 3-28 shows the updated bookmark. As shown, the title of the bookmark is updated. This has been done by passing the following object to the update method: {"title":"Example URL"}.

Searching for Bookmarks

To search bookmarks, use the chrome.bookmarks.search method. This method takes a query and a callback function as its parameters. Query can be made using a string or object. In Listing 3-24, query has been made using a string. If an object were to be used, it would need to have the following properties defined: query, url, and title.

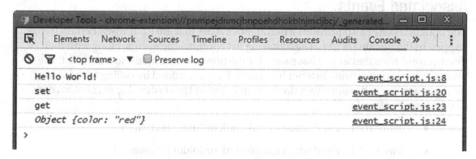

Figure 3-35. *API demos: Storage API*

Using the Bookmarks Hierarchy

The bookmarks API provides the chrome.bookmarks.getTree method to retrieve the entire bookmarks hierarchy. This method takes a function as its only parameter. A bookmark tree is passed as an array to this method. A usage corresponding to this API can be seen in the following code snippet.

Note that the tree is the first element of this passed array. Since this tree is represented using a node, the children property is used to access the nested folders. In this case, the folders are Bookmarks Bar and Other Bookmarks. By iterating over the nested BookmarkTreeNode items (say, using the folder.children.forEach call), you can access all the bookmarks in the hierarchy.

```
chrome.bookmarks.getTree(function(bookmarkTreeAsArray) {
    var bookmarkTree = bookmarkTreeAsArray[0];
    var folders = [];
    if(bookmarkTree.children) {
        bookmarkTree.children.forEach(function(node) {
            if(node.children.length > 0) folders.push(node);
        });
    }
    if(folders.length > 0) {
        folders.forEach(function(folder) {
            folder.children.forEach(function(bookmarkTreeNode) {
                if(bookmarkTreeNode.url) {
                    /*use the node*/
```

```
                }
            }
        }
    }
});
```

Associated Events

The bookmarks API also provides a number of events that are fired when certain things happen to the bookmark tree. The following list contains the events, along with their descriptions. Note that as you have seen for the previous examples, to listen for these events, you need to provide listener functions. They are added by calling addListener on the event. To read more about these events, visit https://developer.chrome.com/extensions/bookmarks.

- onCreated—Fired when a bookmark or folder is created

- onRemoved—Fired when a bookmark or folder is removed

- onChanged—Fired when a bookmark or folder changes

- onMoved—Fired when a bookmark or folder is moved to a different parent folder

- onChildrenReordered—Fired when the children of a folder have changed their order due to the order being sorted in the UI

- onImportBegan—Fired when a bookmark import session begins

- onImportEnded—Fired when a bookmark import session ends

Downloads API

The downloads API (i.e., the chrome.downloads API) is used to programmatically initiate, monitor, manipulate, and search for downloads. It uses the downloads permission. Listing 3-25 contains the code from the DownloadsAPI extension, provided in Chapter 3's Exercise Files folder.

Listing 3-25. Chapter3/DownloadsAPI/event_script.js

```
//region {variables and functions}
var greeting = "Hello World!";
var downloadOptions = {
"url" : "http://www.apress.com/downloadable/download/sample/sample_id/1456/",
"saveAs" : true
};
//end-region
```

```
//region {calls}
console.log(greeting);
chrome.downloads.download(downloadOptions,function(downloadId) {
    console.log(downloadId);
    /*
    chrome.downloads.pause(downloadId,function() {
        if(!chrome.runtime.lastError) console.log("pause");
    });
    */
});
chrome.downloads.onCreated.addListener(function(downloadItem) {
    console.log("onCreated:");
    console.log(downloadItem);
});
chrome.downloads.onErased.addListener(function(downloadId) {
    console.log("onErased:");
    console.log(downloadId);
});
chrome.downloads.onChanged.addListener(function(downloadDelta) {
    console.log("onChanged:");
    console.log(downloadDelta);
});
//end-region
```

Downloading a File

To download a file, use the chrome.downloads.download method. This method takes
two parameters—options (of type object) and callback (of type function). The id
corresponding to the DownloadItem is passed to the callback function. The options
object describes what to download and how. It supports the following properties.

- url (string)

- filename (string)

- saveAs (Boolean)

- method ("GET" or "POST" string)

- headers (array)

- body (string)

■ **Note** DownloadItem is a type associated with the downloads API. This type contains
a long list of properties (details are available at https://developer.chrome.com/
extensions/downloads#type-DownloadItem). Some of the important properties include
id, filename, mime, startTime, endTime, bytesReceived, and totalBytes.

Note that the method, headers, and body properties are to be used if the URL to download uses the HTTPS protocol. Now, let's look at an example to use the download method. For this example, we will download the source code file available at http://www.apress.com/9781430250531. The exact URL of the file to be downloaded is shown in Listing 3-25 (in the downloadOptions object).

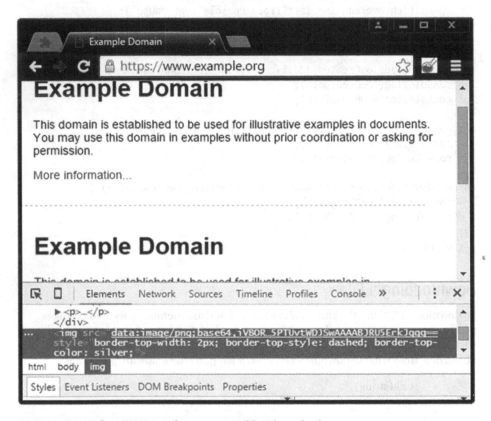

Figure 3-36. *Tabs API: Using the captureVisibleTab method*

As you can see, the call to the download method is made and downloadOptions object is passed as the first argument. The downloadOptions object is defined using the url and saveAs properties. Quite obviously, url is the URL to download. Setting the saveAs property to true is done to use a file chooser to allow the users to select a filename. Note the "Downloaded by" section in Figure 3-29, referring the extension that has initiated the download.

Cancelling or Resuming a Download

Once you have obtained the id corresponding to the DownloadItem (passed to the callback function of the download method), you can easily cancel, resume, or even pause a download. The corresponding calls are very straightforward:

- chrome.downloads.cancel(integer downloadId, function callback)
- chrome.downloads.resume(integer downloadId, function callback)
- chrome.downloads.pause(integer downloadId, function callback)

Opening a Download

Use the open method to open the downloaded file if the DownloadItem is complete. If it is not complete, the open method returns an error through chrome.runtime.lastError. This method only requires a single parameter, which is the downloadId. Note that this method requires an additional permission: downloads.open.

To simply show the downloaded file in its folder in a file manager, a call to the following method needs to be made: chrome.downloads.show(integer downloadId). Moreover, if the only intent is to show the default Downloads folder in a file manager, you need to call the chrome.downloads.showDefaultFolder() method.

Deleting a Download

To remove the downloaded file if the DownloadItem is complete, use the chrome.downloads.removeFile method. This method takes two parameters—downloadId and callback. However, if all that is required is clearing off the download from the history (without deleting the downloaded file), use the chrome.downloads.erase method instead.

This method takes a query object and a callback function as its parameters. The query object can take a long list of properties. Some important ones include id, startedBefore, startedAfter, endedBefore, endedAfter, filenameRegex, and urlRegex. To view the complete list, visit https://developer.chrome.com/extensions/downloads#method-erase.

Associated Events

The downloads API provides some useful events such as onCreated, onChanged, etc., that can be used to provide callbacks when download begins, or when the corresponding DownloadItem's properties change. The following is a list of such events with their descriptions. Note that you can also refer Listing 3-25 to see the exact uses of these events with their listener functions.

- onCreated—Fired with the DownloadItem object when a download begins

- onErased—Fired with the downloadId when a download is erased from history

- onChanged—Fired when any of a DownloadItem's properties change (except bytesReceived and estimatedEndTime)

131

History API

The history API (i.e., the chrome.history API) is used to interact with the browser's record of visited pages. Using this API, you can add, remove, and query for URLs in the browser's history. It uses the history permission. Listing 3-26 contains the code from the HistoryAPI extension, provided in Chapter 3's Exercise Files folder.

Listing 3-26. Chapter3/HistoryAPI/event_script.js

```
//region {variables and functions}
var greeting = "Hello World!";
var tenMinutesAsMilliseconds = 10 * 60 * 1000;
//getTime returns the number of milliseconds since the epoch
var currentTimeAsMilliseconds = new Date().getTime();
//query to filter history using "text", in the past hour
var query = {
    "text" : "apress",
    "startTime" : currentTimeAsMilliseconds - 6 * tenMinutesAsMilliseconds,
    "endTime" : currentTimeAsMilliseconds,
    "maxResults" : 10
};
//end-region

//region {calls}
console.log(greeting);
chrome.history.search(query,function(results) {
    results.forEach(function(result) {
        //result is of type HistoryItem
        console.log(result);
    });
});
chrome.history.getVisits({"url" : "http://www.example.
org"},function(results) {
    results.forEach(function(result) {
        //result is of type VisitItem
        console.log(result);
    });
});
chrome.history.addUrl({"url" : "http://www.example.org"},function() {
    console.log("addUrl");
});
chrome.history.deleteUrl({"url" : "http://www.example.org"},function() {
    console.log("deleteUrl");
});
```

```
/*
chrome.history.deleteAll(function() {
    console.log("deleteAll");
});
*/
//end-region
```

To search the history using a query, use the `chrome.history.search` method. This method takes two parameters—`query` (of type `object`) and `callback` (of type `function`). The `query` object supports the following properties:

- `text`—A free-text query to the history service. Leave it empty to retrieve all pages.

- `startTime`—Limit results to those visited after this date, represented in milliseconds since the epoch.

- `endTime`—Limit results to those visited before this date. Represented in milliseconds since the epoch.

- `maxResults`—The maximum number of results to retrieve. Defaults to 100.

Note that the `callback` function receives an array of `HistoryItem` results. Here, a `HistoryItem` is an object encapsulating one result of a history query. It supports the following useful properties—`id`, `url`, `title`, `lastVisitTime`, `visitCount`, etc.

To retrieve information about visits to a URL, use the `chrome.history.getVisits` method. As shown in Listing 3-26, this method takes an object (with `url` property) as its first parameter. The second parameter is a `callback` function that receives an array of `VisitItem` results.

■ **Note** A `VisitItem` is an object encapsulating one visit to a URL. It is composed of the following properties: `id`, `visitId`, `visitTime`, `referringVisitId`, and `transition` (of `TransitionType`, which describes how the browser navigated to a particular URL). You can read more about the `TransitionType` by visiting `https://developer.chrome.com/extensions/history#transition_types`.

Adding and Removing URLs

To add a URL to the history at the current time, use the `chrome.history.addUrl` method. This method takes two parameters—`details` (of type `object`) and `callback` (of type `function`). The `details` object only supports the `url` property. Similarly, use the `chrome.history.deleteUrl(object details, function callback)` method to remove all occurrences of the given URL from the history. Note that to remove all items from the history, you use the `chrome.history.deleteAll` method. This method only takes a `callback` function as its parameter.

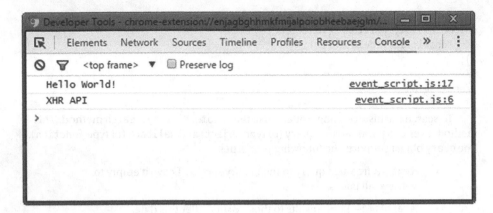

Figure 3-37. *XHRAPI: Logging the response*

Associated Events

The history API supports the onVisited and onVisitRemoved events. The onVisited event is fired when a URL is visited, providing the HistoryItem data for that URL in the corresponding listener function. Note that this event fires before the page has loaded. Similarly, the onVisitRemoved event is fired when one or more URLs are removed from the history service. The listener function corresponding to this event receives an object. This object supports the following properties:

- allHistory (Boolean)-True if all history was removed. If it's true, URLs will be empty.

- urls (array)-String array of removed URLs.

Notifications API

You can use the chrome.notifications API to create rich notifications using templates and show these notifications to users in the system tray. It uses the notifications permission. Listing 3-27 contains the code from the NotificationsAPI extension, provided in Chapter 3's Exercise Files folder.

Listing 3-27. Chapter3/NotificationsAPI/event_script.js

```
//region {variables and functions}
var greeting = "Hello World!";
var title = "NotificationsAPI";
var message = "Test message X";
var oneMinuteAsMilliseconds = 1 * 60 * 1000;
//getTime returns the number of milliseconds since the epoch
var currentTimeAsMilliseconds = new Date().getTime();
```

```
var notificationId = "myNotification1";
var NOTIFICATION_TEMPLATE_TYPE = {
    BASIC : "basic",
    IMAGE : "image",
    LIST : "list",
    PROGRESS : "progress"
};
var myButton1 = {
    title : "Click X",
    iconUrl : "button.png"
};
var myButton2 = {
    title : "Click Y",
    iconUrl : "button.png"
};
var myItem1 = {
    title : "Item X",
    message : "This is item X"
};
var myItem2 = {
    title : "Item Y",
    message : "This is item Y"
};
var notificationOptions = {
    type : NOTIFICATION_TEMPLATE_TYPE.LIST,
    iconUrl : "icon.png",
    title : title,
    message : message,
    eventTime : currentTimeAsMilliseconds + oneMinuteAsMilliseconds,
    buttons : [myButton1,myButton2],
    /*imageUrl : "icon.png",*/
    items : [myItem1,myItem2], //comment out for BASIC
    /*progress : 0,*/
    isClickable : true
};
//end-region

//region {calls}
console.log(greeting);
chrome.notifications.create(notificationId,notificationOptions,
    function(id) {
        console.log("create: " + id);
    }
);
/*
```

```
chrome.notifications.clear(notificationId,function(wasCleared) {
    console.log("clear: " + wasCleared);
});
*/
/*
chrome.notifications.getAll(function(notifications) {
    console.log("getAll:");
    console.log(notifications);
});
*/
chrome.notifications.onClicked.addListener(function(id) { //notification-id
    console.log("onClicked: " + id);
    notificationOptions.title = title + " (onClicked)";
    chrome.notifications.update(notificationId,notificationOptions,
        function(wasUpdated) {
            console.log("update: " + wasUpdated);
        }
    );
});
chrome.notifications.onClosed.addListener(function(notificationId,byUser) {
    console.log("onClosed: " + notificationId);
});
chrome.notifications.onButtonClicked.addListener(
    function(notificationId,buttonIndex) {
        console.log("onButtonClicked: " + buttonIndex);
    }
);
//end-region
```

Creating and Clearing a Notification

To create a notification, use the chrome.notifications.create method. This method
takes three parameters-notificationId (of type string), notificationOptions (of type
object), and a callback function. Note that the notificationOptions object describes
the contents of the notification. The complete list of properties it supports is available at
https://developer.chrome.com/apps/notifications#type-NotificationOptions.

An important property (in the notificationOptions object) called type declares the
template to be used for creating a notification. Other properties such as title, message,
buttons, imageUrl, items, progress, etc. define the specific parts of the template.
Figures 3-30 to 3-32 contain examples of different notification templates. In Listing 3-27,
note the NOTIFICATION_TEMPLATE_TYPE object used as an enum to select the notification
template.

You can clear a notification by calling the chrome.notifications.clear method,
which takes the notificationId as its parameter. To clear all the notifications, use the
clear method, along with the chrome.notifications.getAll method, which takes a
callback function as its parameter. This callback receives an object consisting of all the
notifications.

Updating a Notification

To update an existing notification, use the chrome.notifications.update method. This method takes three parameters-notificationId (of type string), notificationOptions (of type object), and a callback function. The callback function receives a Boolean argument indicating whether the notification updated. In Listing 3-27, note that the update method is called from within the listener function for the onClicked event.

Associated Events

The notifications API supports the onClosed, onClicked, and onButtonClicked events. The onClosed event is fired when the notification is closed-either by the system or by user action. As seen in Listing 3-27, the listener function corresponding to this event receives two arguments-(string) notificationId and (Boolean) byUser.

The onButtonClicked event is fired when the user clicks a button (see Figure 3-34) in the notification. Note that buttons are provided using the buttons property in the notificationOptions object (see Listing 3-27). The listener function for this event receives the notificationId as well as the buttonIndex. Similarly, the onClicked event is fired when the user clicks in a non-button area of the notification. This event is used in Listing 3-27 to update the notification's title property (see Figure 3-33).

Storage API

The storage API (i.e., the chrome.storage API) is used to store, retrieve, and track changes to user data. It uses the storage permission. Listing 3-28 contains the code from the StorageAPI extension, provided in Chapter 3's Exercise Files folder. This API is optimized to meet the specific storage needs of extensions. It provides the same storage capabilities as the localStorage API with the following key differences:

- User data can be automatically synced with Chrome sync (using chrome.storage.sync API).

- Your extension's content scripts can directly access user data without the need for a *background page*.

- It's asynchronous with bulk read and write operations, and therefore faster than the blocking and serial localStorage API.

- User data can be stored as objects (the localStorage API stores data in strings).

Sync versus Local Storage

To store user data for your extension, you can use the storage.sync or storage.local APIs. When using storage.sync, the stored data will automatically be synced to any Chrome browser that the user is logged into, provided the user has sync enabled.

When Chrome is offline, Chrome stores the data locally. The next time the browser is online, Chrome syncs the data. Even if a user disables syncing, the storage.sync API will still work. In this case, it will behave identically to the storage.local API.

■ **Note**   Confidential user information should not be stored! The storage area isn't encrypted.

Listing 3-28. Chapter3/StorageAPI/event_script.js

```
//region {variables and functions}
var greeting = "Hello World!";
//end-region

//region {calls}
console.log(greeting);
/*
//single key or a list of keys for items to remove
chrome.storage.sync.remove("color",function() {
    console.log("remove");
    chrome.storage.sync.get("color",function(items) {
        console.log("get");
        console.log(items);
    });
});
*/
chrome.storage.sync.set({"color":"red"},function() {
    console.log("set");
    //string or array of string or object keys
    chrome.storage.sync.get("color",function(items) {
        console.log("get");
        console.log(items);
    });
});
chrome.storage.onChanged.addListener(function(changes,areaName) {
    console.log(changes);
    //"sync","local" or "managed"
    console.log(areaName);
});
//end-region
```

Setting and Getting Items

You set and get items from storage using the following API calls respectively-chrome. storage.sync.set, and chrome.storage.sync.get. The get method takes a string, an array of strings, or object keys as its first parameter, and the set method takes an object (with key-value pairs) as its first parameter. The second parameter in the get method is a callback function, and it receives an object as its argument. Figure 3-35 contains the corresponding logs from these method calls.

Removing Items

You can easily remove an item in storage by calling the chrome.storage.sync.remove method. This method takes a string or array of strings as its first parameter, and an optional callback function as its second parameter. To remove all items from the storage, use the chrome.storage.sync.clear method.

Associated Events

The storage API provides the chrome.storage.onChanged event. This event is fired when one or more (storage) items change. The listener function corresponding to this event receives two arguments-(object) changes and (string) areaName. Here, areaName is name of the storage area (sync, local, etc.).

Tabs API

The tabs API (i.e., the chrome.tabs API) is used to interact with the browser's tab system. You can use this API to create, modify, and rearrange tabs in the browser. It uses the tabs permission. Listing 3-29 contains the code from the TabsAPI extension, provided in Chapter 3's Exercise Files folder. You have already used the query, connect, sendMessage, executeScript, and insertCSS methods from this API. This section looks at the remaining methods.

■ **Note**   You can use most chrome.tabs methods and events without declaring any permissions in the extension's manifest file. However, if you require access to the url, title, or favIconUrl properties of tabs.Tab, you must declare the tabs permission in the manifest.

Listing 3-29. Chapter3/TabsAPI/event_script.js

```javascript
//region {variables and functions}
var greeting = "Hello World!";
var createProperties = {
    url : "http://www.example.org",
    active : false,
};
var updateProperties = {
    pinned : true
};
function getJavaScriptCode(dataUrl) {
    var javascriptCode = "var imgElement = document.createElement('img');";
    javascriptCode += "document.body.appendChild(imgElement);";
    javascriptCode += "imgElement.style.borderTop = '2px dashed silver';";
    javascriptCode += "imgElement.src = ";
    javascriptCode += "'" + dataUrl + "';";
    return javascriptCode;
}
function createAndUpdateTab(tab) {
    chrome.tabs.create(createProperties,function(tab) {
        console.log("create");
        //integer or array of integers
        //chrome.tabs.remove(tab.id);
        /*
        chrome.tabs.duplicate(tab.id,function(tab) {
            console.log("duplicate");
        });
        */
        chrome.tabs.update(tab.id,updateProperties,function(tab) {
            console.log("update");
            //chrome.tabs.reload(tab.id);
            chrome.tabs.getZoom(tab.id,function(zoomFactor) {
                console.log("getZoom");
                console.log(zoomFactor); //1
            });
            /*
            chrome.tabs.setZoom(tab.id,2,function() {
                console.log("setZoom");
            });
            */
        });
    });
}
//end-region
```

```
//region {calls}
console.log(greeting);
chrome.browserAction.onClicked.addListener(function(tab) {
    chrome.tabs.captureVisibleTab({"format":"png"},function(dataUrl) {
        //Cannot access a chrome:// URL

chrome.tabs.executeScript(tab.id,{"code":getJavaScriptCode(dataUrl)});
    });
    //createAndUpdateTab(tab);
});
//end-region
```

Creating and Removing a Tab

To create a tab, use the chrome.tabs.create method. This method takes two
parameters-createProperties (of type object) and callback (of type function). The
createProperties object supports the following useful properties-index, url, active,
and pinned. The callback function receives an argument of type Tab (tabs.Tab). A tab
can also be duplicated by calling the chrome.tabs.duplicate method, as shown in
Listing 3-29 (see the commented-out section in the createAndUpdateTab function).

Use the chrome.tabs.remove method to close one or more tabs. This method takes
the ID of the tab to close, or a list of such IDs as its first parameter. It also supports an
optional callback function as its second parameter.

Updating a Tab

Use the chrome.tabs.update method to modify the properties of a tab. This method takes
three parameters-tabId, updateProperties, and callback. As you might have guessed,
tabId is the ID of the tab to update. The callback function receives the details of the
updated tab via the tab argument. The updateProperties object specifies the properties
to update. Only the following properties are supported-url, active, highlighted,
pinned, muted, and openerTabId. Note that you can also reload a tab by calling the
chrome.tabs.reload method. This method takes the ID of the tab to reload as its first
parameter and an optional callback function as its second parameter.

Listing 3-30. Chapter3/TabsAPI/manifest.json

```
{
    "manifest_version" : 2,
    "name" : "API Demos: tabs API",
    "description" : "Demonstrates use of the tabs API",
    "version" : "1.2",
    "background" : {
        "scripts" : ["event_script.js"],
        "persistent" : false
    },
    "browser_action" : {
```

```
        "default_icon" : "icon.png"
    },
    "permissions" : [
        "tabs",
        "<all_urls>"
    ]
}
```

■ **Note**   To zoom a specified tab, use the `chrome.tabs.setZoom` method. Additionally, to get the current zoom factor of a specified tab, use the `chrome.tabs.getZoom` method.

Capturing a Tab

To capture the visible area of the currently active tab in the specified window, use the `chrome.tabs.captureVisibleTab` method. This method takes three parameters-`windowId`, `options`, and `callback`. The `windowId` parameter is optional, and it defaults to the current window. The `options` parameter is used to specify the format of the image. The `callback` function receives the `dataUrl` (string) argument-which is a URL referring to the data containing the encoded image of the visible area of the captured tab. Note that the `dataUrl` can be assigned to the `src` property of an HTML `img` element, as shown in Listing 3-29. An image corresponding to this is shown in Figure 3-36. Also note that this method requires an additional permission-`<all_urls>`—shown in Listing 3-30.

Associated Events

The `chrome.tabs` API provides a long list of events corresponding to almost every available method. For example, the `onCreated`, `onUpdated`, `onRemoved`, `onZoomChange`, etc., events. The complete list of such events is available at `https://developer.chrome.com/extensions/tabs`.

XHR API

An extension can talk to remote servers (using the `XMLHttpRequest` object) by requesting cross-origin permissions. Such permissions are requested with the help of *match patterns* that provide access to one or more hosts (see "`*://localhost/*`" in Listing 3-31).

Listing 3-31. Chapter3/XHRAPI/manifest.json

```
{
    "manifest_version" : 2,
    "name" : "API Demos: xhr API",
    "description" : "Demonstrates use of the xhr API",
    "version" : "1.2",
    "background" : {
        "scripts" : ["event_script.js"],
```

```
        "persistent" : false
    },
    "permissions" : [
        "*://localhost/*"
    ]
}
```

Once the host permission is requested, the XHR API can be used, similarly to the way it is used in regular web pages. In Listing 3-32, note that the ucService (PHP script to uppercase the input string) is served from my local HTTP server. The PHP script is available in Listing 3-33.

Listing 3-32. Chapter3/XHRAPI/event_script.js

```javascript
//region {variables and functions}
var greeting = "Hello World!";
var xhr = new XMLHttpRequest();
function onReadyStateChange() {
    if(xhr.readyState == 4) {
        console.log(xhr.responseText);
    }
}
var host = "http://localhost/";
var ucService = host + "Exercise Files/Chapter3/XHRAPI/webpage.php?";
var queryString = "name=" + encodeURIComponent("xhr api");
//end-region

//region {calls}
console.log(greeting);
xhr.onreadystatechange = onReadyStateChange;
xhr.open("GET",ucService + queryString);
xhr.send();
//end-region
```

The query string "name=xhr api" is provided in a static manner. It could be dynamically provided in your extension, for example, from a Browser-Action popup, or Content-UI, etc. Figure 3-37 shows the corresponding response from the server.

Listing 3-33. Chapter3/XHRAPI/WebServer/webpage.php

```php
<?php
$raw_input = trim($_GET["name"]);
if(!preg_match("/^[a-zA-Z ]*$/",$raw_input)) {
    echo "";
} else {
    echo strtoupper($raw_input);
}
?>
```

Summary

The beginning of this chapter discussed the left-out input components from the previous chapter-omnibox input, context menu item, and Content-UI. After this, you learned the various ways in which scripting components can interact with each other using the messaging APIs provided by the Google Chrome Extensions framework. In addition to this, you also learned how ordinary web pages can interact with an extension.

You then learned what permission strings are in a manifest file, before learning about how to use the many useful APIs provided by the Extensions framework. You also learned how using XHR in an extension is possible across different origins using *match pattern* permission strings in the manifest file.

In the next chapter, you will read about a few remaining features provided by the Chrome Extensions framework, such as themes, override pages (to override a new tab, bookmarks page, etc.), and options pages, which enable you to enhance the niche of your extension on the Chrome browser.

CHAPTER 4

■ ■ ■

More About Extensions

By now you have learned about most of the features of Google Chrome Extensions, including the architecture, messaging between different components, and the APIs provided by the Google Chrome Extensions framework. This chapter covers the remaining features of Google Chrome Extensions, such as the options page, override pages, and themes. In addition to this, you will learn about some security concerns that you should keep in mind when developing Google Chrome Extensions. These include API permissions, *match pattern* permissions, content-script injections, etc.

Providing an Options Page

You can allow users to customize the behavior of the extension by providing an options page (see Figure 4-4). An important point to note is that such a provision can be easily made without the use of an options page. This can be done, for example, by providing a popup component consisting of a UI to allow saving of preferences for the extension (say using the chrome.storage API). However, this is not recommended, as it won't allow users to access the options page from the Extensions Management page (see Figure 4-3 for the options link).

Role of Manifest for this Component

To declare an options page, you need to use the options_ui manifest attribute. This attribute supports the following properties. As seen in Listing 4-1 (from the OverridePages extension), the page and chrome_style properties suffice to declare the options page for an extension.

- page (string)—The path to the options page, relative to the extension's root.

- chrome_style (boolean)—If true, a Chrome user agent stylesheet will be applied to the options page. The default value is false, but for a consistent UI with Chrome, it is recommended to set this value to true.

© Prateek Mehta 2016
P. Mehta, *Creating Google Chrome Extensions*, DOI 10.1007/978-1-4842-1775-7_4

- open_in_tab (boolean)—If true, the extension's options page will be opened in a new tab rather than embedded in chrome://extensions. The default value is false, and true is not recommended.

Listing 4-1. Chapter4/OverridePages/manifest.json

```json
{
    "name" : "My New-Tab",
    "version" : "1.2",
    "manifest_version" : 2,
    "chrome_url_overrides" : {
        /*newtab,history,bookmarks*/
        "newtab" : "myNewTab.html"
    },
    "permissions" : ["bookmarks","storage"],
    /*Using an options page*/
    "options_ui" : {
        "page" : "myOptionsPage.html",
        /*Use Chrome stylesheet*/
        "chrome_style" : true
    }
}
```

Writing an Options Page

An options page is made entirely of an HTML page (displayed in Figure 4-4). Listing 4-2 contains the HTML code for the options page used in the OverridePages extension. This extension is available in Chapter 4's Exercise Files folder. As described, it is recommended to use the Chrome stylesheet for this HTML, by setting the chrome_style property to true in the manifest.

■ **Note** To programmatically open an options page, use the chrome.runtime. openOptionsPage method.

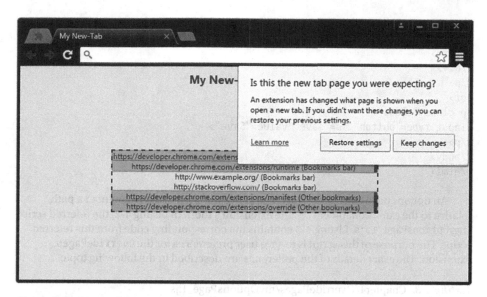

Figure 4-1. *New Tab page: override prompt*

Listing 4-2. Chapter4/OverridePages/myOptionsPage.html

```
<!DOCTYPE html>
<html>
<head>
<title>My Options-Page</title>
<script src="myOptionsPage_1.js"></script>
<style>
div.left {
float:left;
}
div.right {
float:right;
}
p.clear {
clear:both;
}
</style>
</head>
<body>
<p>
<div class="left">
Only display matching bookmarks?
</div>
<div class="right">
<form>
```

```
<input type="radio" name="highlight" value="1"> Yes
<input type="radio" name="highlight" value="0" checked="checked"> No
</form>
</div>
</p>
<br>
<p class="clear">
<input type="button" id="save" value="Save">
</p>
</body>
</html>
```

An options page can refer scripts. The src of the script needs to point to a path, relative to the extension folder (i.e., the extension's root). In Listing 4-2, the referred script is myOptionsPage_1.js. Listing 4-3 contains the corresponding code from this referred script. The purpose of this script is to save user preferences for the OverridePages extension. The exact details of the preference are described in the following topic.

Listing 4-3. Chapter4/OverridePages/myOptionsPage_1.js

```
//region {variables and functions}
var storageKey = "APPEND_MATCHING_ONLY";
var items = {};
var saveButtonID = "save";
function logSuccess(task) {
    console.log("%s Successful!",task);
}
//end-region

//region {calls}
document.addEventListener("DOMContentLoaded",function(dcle) {
    var saveButton = document.getElementById(saveButtonID);
    saveButton.addEventListener("click",function(ce) {
        if(document.forms[0].highlight.value == "1") {
            items[storageKey] = true;
            chrome.storage.sync.set(
                items,
                function() {
                    if(!chrome.runtime.lastError)
                        logSuccess("Set-Storage");
                }
            );
        } else {
            items[storageKey] = false;
            chrome.storage.sync.set(
                items,
                function() {
```

```
            if(!chrome.runtime.lastError)
                logSuccess("Set-Storage");
        }
    );
    }
});
});
//end-region
```

Working with Override Pages

Override pages are a way to substitute (i.e., override) an HTML file from the extension for a page that Google Chrome normally provides. In addition to HTML, an override page usually has CSS and JavaScript code. An extension can override any one of the following pages:

- *Bookmark Manager* (chrome://bookmarks)—The page that appears when the user chooses the Bookmark Manager menu item from the Chrome menu or, on a Mac, the Bookmark Manager item from the Bookmarks menu.

- *History* (chrome://history)—The page that appears when the user chooses the History menu item from the Chrome menu or, on a Mac, the Show Full History item from the History menu.

- *New Tab* (chrome://newtab)—The page that appears when the user creates a new tab or window.

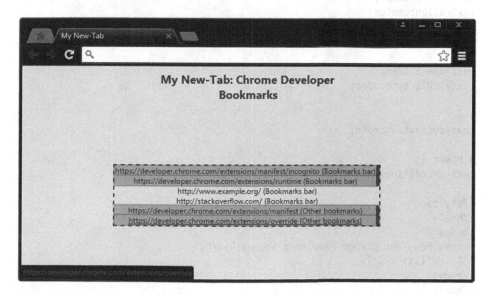

Figure 4-2. New Tab page with bookmarks

■ **Note**   An extension can override only one page. For example, the `OverridePages`
extension, provided in the `Exercise Files` folder, overrides the New Tab page.

Listing 4-4. Chapter4/OverridePages/myNewTab.html

```html
<!DOCTYPE html>
<html>
<head>
<title>My New-Tab</title>
<script src="myNewTab_1.js"></script>
<style>
body {
background-color:#eee;
}
h2 {
width:50%;
margin:auto auto;
text-align:center;
color:#555;
}
ul {
padding:0px;
width:60%;
margin-left:auto;
margin-right:auto;
margin-top:100px;
text-align:center;
border:2px dashed #555;
}
li {
overflow:hidden;
list-style-type:none;
}
a {
text-decoration:none;
}
a:hover {
text-decoration:underline;
}
</style>
</head>
<body>
<h2>My New-Tab: Chrome Developer Bookmarks</h2>
<ul id="list"></ul>
</body>
</html>
```

Role of Manifest for this Component

To override a page, use the chrome_url_overrides manifest attribute. The exact page that will be overridden is specified using the bookmarks, history, or newtab property. An example for this is shown in Listing 4-1, where the New Tab page is overridden by specifying "newtab" : "myNewTab.html". Listing 4-4 contains the corresponding HTML code from the myNewTab.html file.

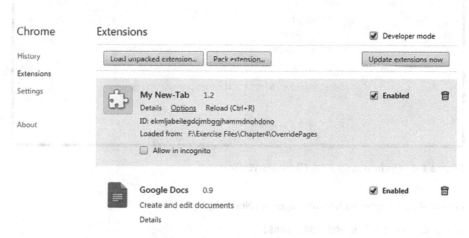

Figure 4-3. *Extensions Management page: options link*

OverridePages Extension

The OverridePages extension provided in the Exercise Files folder of this chapter can override the New Tab page. You can load this extension in your browser for testing. Note the prompt that appears upon loading this extension (see Figure 4-1). This is required by the Chrome browser to know if the override is intended (by the user) or not.

As seen in Figure 4-2, this extension overrides the New Tab page to display the bookmarks. The referred script myNewTab_1.js is used to append bookmark items to the HTML ul element list, seen in Listing 4-4 as <ul id="list"></ul>. Listings 4-5 and 4-6 contain the JavaScript code from the referred script.

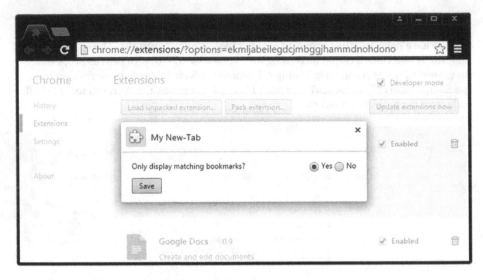

Figure 4-4. *Options page with Chrome stylesheet*

Listing 4-5. Chapter4/OverridePages/myNewTab_1.js

```
//region {variables and functions}
var folders = [];
var listName = "list";
var host = "developer.chrome.com";
var itemBorderRightStyle = "5px solid #666";
var itemBoxShadowStyle = "0px 0px 2px #333";
var itemBackgroundColor = "#ccc";
var storageKey = "APPEND_MATCHING_ONLY";
function appendItem(listElement,nodeURL,nodeParentTitle) {
    var li = document.createElement("li");
    var a = document.createElement("a");
    a.href = nodeURL;
    a.innerText = nodeURL + " (" + nodeParentTitle + ")";
    li.appendChild(a);
    if(nodeURL.indexOf(host) != -1) {
        li.style.borderRight = itemBorderRightStyle;
        li.style.boxShadow = itemBoxShadowStyle;
        li.style.backgroundColor = itemBackgroundColor;
    }
    listElement.appendChild(li);
}
function appendMatchingItem(listElement,nodeURL,nodeParentTitle) {
    if(nodeURL.indexOf(host) != -1)
        appendItem(listElement,nodeURL,nodeParentTitle);
}
```

```
function populateList(listElement) {
    folders.forEach(function(folder) {
        folder.children.forEach(function(bookmarkTreeNode) {
            appendItem(listElement,bookmarkTreeNode.url,folder.title);
        });
    });
}
function populateListV2(listElement) {
    chrome.storage.sync.get(storageKey,function(items) {
        if(!chrome.runtime.lastError && items[storageKey]) {
            folders.forEach(function(folder) {
                folder.children.forEach(function(bookmarkTreeNode) {
                    if(bookmarkTreeNode.url)
                        appendMatchingItem(
                            listElement,
                            bookmarkTreeNode.url,
                            folder.title
                        );
                });
            });
        } else {
            folders.forEach(function(folder) {
                folder.children.forEach(function(bookmarkTreeNode) {
                    if(bookmarkTreeNode.url)
                        appendItem(
                            listElement,
                            bookmarkTreeNode.url,
                            folder.title
                        );
                });
            });
        }
    });
}
//end-region
```

To display bookmarks in the New Tab page, the bookmarks API (i.e., the `chrome.bookmarks` API) has been used. Recall from Chapter 3 that each node in the bookmark tree is represented by a `bookmarks.BookmarkTreeNode` object. And also recall that to retrieve the entire bookmark's hierarchy, you need to use the `chrome.bookmarks.getTree` method.

In Listing 4-6, note the use of the `children.length` property to access the child bookmark nodes. All these bookmark nodes are stored in the `folders` array. Listing 4-5 contains the `populateList` and `populateListV2` functions. Any of these functions can be used to append bookmark items to the aforementioned HTML `ul` element `list`. These bookmark items are obtained from the `folders` array.

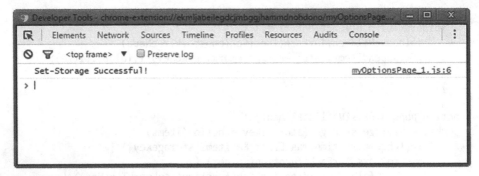

Figure 4-5. *Options page: logging on to the console*

The OverridePages extension contains an options page to save a user preference to only allow display of matching bookmarks in the New Tab page (here, a matched bookmark has an URL belonging to a certain host). To implement this, the storage API (i.e., the chrome.storage API) has been used. In Listing 4-3, note the use of chrome.storage.sync.set method to save the selected option (the Yes and No options can be seen in Figure 4-4). Also note that the log corresponding to this call can be seen in Figure 4-5. In Listings 4-3 and 4-5, the key corresponding to the storage item (for the selected option) is declared in the following way:

```
var storageKey = "APPEND_MATCHING_ONLY";
```

To make use of this stored item (which corresponds to the selected option—Yes or No), the populateListV2 function calls the chrome.storage.sync.get method. If no runtime error is caused during this call, and the storage item is set to true (i.e., Yes), the appendMatchingItem function is called. Otherwise, the appendItem function is called. Before appending a bookmark item, the appendMatchingItem function tests if the bookmark node to append has the URL that matches the host developer.chrome.com. The corresponding output is shown in Figure 4-6.

Listing 4-6. Chapter4/OverridePages/myNewTab_1.js

```
//region {calls}
document.addEventListener("DOMContentLoaded",function(dcle) {
      var listElement = document.getElementById(listName);
      chrome.bookmarks.getTree(function(bookmarkTreeAsArray) {
            var bookmarkTree = bookmarkTreeAsArray[0];
            if(bookmarkTree.children) {
                  bookmarkTree.children.forEach(function(node) {
                        if(node.children.length > 0) folders.push(node);
                  });
            }
            //populateList(listElement);
            populateListV2(listElement);
      });
});
//end-region
```

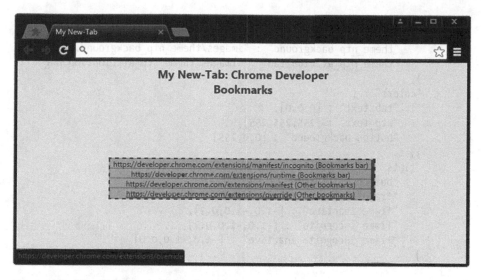

Figure 4-6. *New Tab page with bookmarks*

Creating Themes for Google Chrome

A theme is a special kind of extension that changes the way the browser looks. Themes are packaged like regular extensions, but note that *themes don't contain JavaScript or HTML code.* You can try out the themes available on the Chrome Web Store. The following URL will take you directly to the themes category: `https://chrome.google.com/webstore/category/themes`.

■ **Note** There is no difference in uploading extensions or themes to the dashboard, because a theme is also an extension.

Creating a theme is extremely easy, as it only requires few images and a bunch of lines in the manifest file to create it. Figure 4-7 displays the images used in the Themes extension, which are provided in Chapter 4's `Exercise Files` folder. Listing 4-7 contains the code from the manifest file corresponding to this extension.

Listing 4-7. Chapter4/Themes/manifest.json

```
{
    "manifest_version" : 2,
    "name" : "HelloTheme",
    "version" : "1.2",
    "theme" : {
        "images" : {
```

```
            "theme_frame" : "images/theme_frame_golden.png",
            "theme_toolbar" : "images/theme_toolbar_silver.png",
            "theme_ntp_background" : "images/theme_ntp_background.png",
            "theme_ntp_attribution" : "images/theme_ntp_attribution.png"
        },
        "colors" : {
            "tab_text" : [0,0,0],
            "ntp_text" : [255,255,255],
            "button_background" : [0,0,255]
        },
        "tints" : {
            "buttons" : [0.0,0.0,0.0],
            "frame" : [-1.0,-1.0,-1.0],
            "frame_inactive" : [-1.0,-1.0,0.3],
            "frame_incognito" : [-1.0,-1.0,0.2],
            "frame_incognito_inactive" : [-1.0,-1.0,0.0]
        }
    }
}
```

Figure 4-7. *Images used for the Themes extension*

■ **Note**   The SVG file has been provided in the `Exercise Files` folder so you can customize the shapes used to create the images for the theme.

A theme supports the `image`, `color`, and `tint` elements. To create a theme, you need to define these elements for the `theme` manifest attribute (see Listing 4-7). In addition to this, you also need to define the properties corresponding to these elements. Some of the most useful properties are listed here, along with their descriptions.

- `theme_frame`—The frame of the window, i.e., the area that is behind the tabs.

- `theme_toolbar`—The theme for the current tab and the toolbar together.

- `theme_ntp_background`—The background image for the New Tab page.

- `theme_ntp_attribution`—The attribution image for the New Tab page.

- `tab_text`—The color of the text in the title of current tab.

- `ntp_text`—The color of all the text in the New Tab page.

- `button_background`—The background color of all the window buttons (for example, minimize, close, etc.)

- `buttons`—The color tint that can be applied to various buttons in the Chrome toolbar.

- `frame`—The color tint that can be applied to the frame of Chrome.

- `frame_inactive`—The color tint that is applied when the Chrome window is inactive.

- `frame_incognito`—The color tint to the frame in incognito mode.

- `frame_incognito_inactive`—Same as with `frame_incognito`, but when the window is inactive (and in incognito mode).

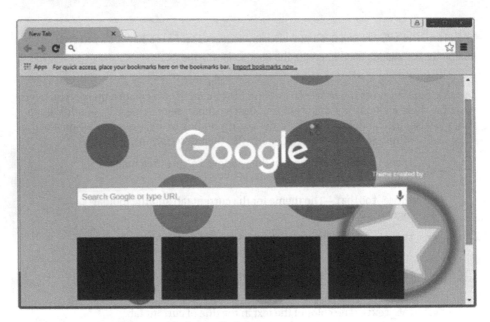

Figure 4-8. *New Tab page with the applied theme*

■ **Note**   Themes don't contain JavaScript or HTML code.

Figure 4-8 displays the New Tab page with the applied theme. Note the golden colored frame of the window, as specified using the theme_frame attribute. Also note the background image for the New Tab page. It is specified using the theme_ntp_background attribute. To specify an attribution image, use the theme_ntp_attribution attribute. In the provided extension, the attribution image is theme_ntp_attribution.png, which is the circular image with a yellow logo (seen in Figure 4-8 in the lower-right corner).

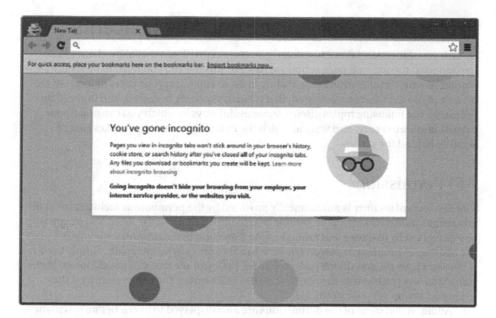

Figure 4-9. *Theme in incognito mode*

■ **Note**   Tints are in Hue-Saturation-Lightness (HSL) format, using floating-point numbers in the range 0 to 1.0. A value of -1.0 is for no change.

For the incognito mode, you can apply color tints to existing styles. For example, in Figure 4-9 note the color tint applied to the window frame. This tint is applied using the `frame_incognito` attribute (see Listing 4-7). Similarly, color tints can also be applied to different styles for the inactive mode. In Figure 4-10, note the difference between the active window (in the front) and the inactive window (the inactive window is in back and has a darker frame).

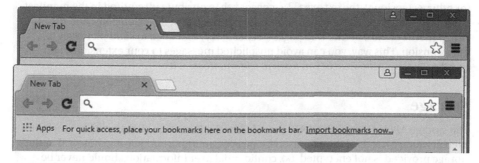

Figure 4-10. *Color tint for inactive window (back window)*

Extensions Development: Security Concerns

By now you understand that extensions have certain privileges that allow them to go beyond what regular web page scripts can do. For this reason, you need to be security conscious when writing extensions. Failing to do so can affect your users in terms of the privacy of the data that was accessed, that is currently being accessed, and that will be accessed. The following topics discuss some useful ways in which you can make your extensions more secure, and ways in which the Extensions framework takes care of security behind the scenes.

API Permissions

The first level of security is automatically provided by the permissions architecture in the Extensions framework. API permissions help to limit damage if the extension or app is compromised by malware. For example, if an extension that manipulates bookmarks has the `bookmarks` permission, it won't be able to affect the user's downloads, simply because it does not have the `downloads` permission. So, here you see that you should *never request unnecessary permissions in the manifest,* as this will weaken the user's security if the extension or app gets compromised.

Additionally, some of the permissions are also displayed to users, before installation of the extension (or app), as a warning. Note that you can read more about these warnings at the following URL: `https://developer.chrome.com/extensions/permission_warnings`.

Match Pattern Permissions

Similar to the permissions for APIs, *match patterns* provide access to one or more hosts (for use with the XHR API). To prevent damage to the extension or to the user's security, you should *only allow white-listed hosts in your extensions,* or in fact, the exact white-listed remote service that your extension needs to use.

Externally Connectable

As discussed previously in the "Web Page Scripts and Event Scripts" section (in Chapter 3), for an extension to be able to receive messages from external web pages (or other extensions), the `externally_connectable` attribute is required in the manifest. For the `ids` and `matches` keys, you should specify the IDs of the extensions, and the URL patterns of the external web pages (respectively) that need to send messages to the extension. This way, you can avoid unsolicited messages to your extensions, and *specifically choose the sources you want to communicate with.*

Storage

The storage API is an optimized API provided by the Extensions framework to meet the specific storage needs of the extensions. However, an important point to note is that the storage provided is not encrypted. So, confidential user information should never be stored using this API.

To store user data for your extension, you can use `storage.sync` or `storage.local`. When using `storage.sync`, the stored data will automatically be synced to any Chrome browser that the user is logged in to, provided the user has sync enabled.

When Chrome is offline, Chrome stores the data locally. The next time the browser is online, Chrome syncs the data. Even if a user disables syncing, `storage.sync` will still work. In this case, it will behave identically to `storage.local`.

To use the `storage.sync` API, the following calls need to be made. To read more about this API, you can refer back to the topic "Storage API" in the previous chapter.

```
chrome.storage.sync.get(string or array of string or object keys, function
callback)
chrome.storage.sync.set(object items, function callback)
```

Content Script

When writing a content script, you should be aware of two security issues. First, be careful not to introduce security vulnerabilities into the web page your content script is injected into. For example, if your content script receives data from a remote server (for example, via the XHR API), be careful to filter that data for cross-site scripting attacks before injecting it into the current web page. For example, it's better to inject data via `innerText` rather than `innerHTML`.

■ **Note**   Content scripts execute in a special environment called an *isolated world*. They have access to the DOM of the web page they are injected into, but not to any JavaScript variables or functions created by the web page. It looks to each content script as if there is no other JavaScript executing on the web page it is running on. The same is true in reverse: JavaScript running on the web page cannot call any functions or access any variables defined by content scripts. Isolated worlds allow each content script to make changes to its JavaScript environment without worrying about conflicting with the web page or with other content scripts.

It's worth noting what happens with JavaScript objects that are shared by the web page and the extension—for example, the `window.onload` event. Each isolated world sees its own version of the object. Assigning to the object affects your independent copy of the object. For example, both the web page and extension can assign to `window.onload`, but neither one can read the other's event handler. The event handlers are called in the order in which they were assigned.

Second, although running your content script in an isolated world provides some protection from the web page, a malicious web page (or remote service, accessed via the XHR API) might still be able to attack your content script if you use data from the web page (or service) indiscriminately. For example, using the eval method to parse this data allows it to be executed, enabling malicious code to execute from within your extension. To avoid this, *choose safer (parsing) APIs that do not execute code,* such as the JSON.parse method.

Summary

This chapter discussed the remaining features of Google Chrome Extensions, such as options page, override pages, and themes. The OverridePages extension described in this chapter overrides the New Tab page. The use of an options page was also demonstrated in this extension. This page provided a single option to save a user preference for the OverridePages extension.

The Themes extension displayed a simple theme for the browser—providing colored frames for the window, a background image for the New Tab page, and color tints for the incognito and inactive windows. Finally, some security concerns were described, and their corresponding remedies were also discussed. The issues that were described included API permissions, *match pattern* permissions, the externally_connectable attribute, storage, and content-script injection.

This chapter concludes the book. You discovered what Google Chrome Extensions are, learned how to create them, learned about extension components and messaging, and publishing of extensions on the Chrome Web Store (formerly the Google Chrome Extensions Gallery). So now it's time for you to leverage the power of the Google Chrome browser by creating your own awesome extensions!

Index

■ D

■ E, F

■ H

■ I, J, K, L

■ M, N

■ O

Get the eBook for only $5!

Why limit yourself?

Now you can take the weightless companion with you wherever you go and access your content on your PC, phone, tablet, or reader.

Since you've purchased this print book, we're happy to offer you the eBook in all 3 formats for just $5.

Convenient and fully searchable, the PDF version enables you to easily find and copy code—or perform examples by quickly toggling between instructions and applications. The MOBI format is ideal for your Kindle, while the ePUB can be utilized on a variety of mobile devices.

To learn more, go to www.apress.com/companion or contact support@apress.com.

Printed in the United States
By Bookmasters

Printed in the United States
By Bookmasters